THE LITTLE HISTORY OF

THE
TEDDY
BEAR

*In memory of teddy bear enthusiast
Pauline Grattan*

THE LITTLE HISTORY OF

THE
TEDDY
BEAR

MICHÈLE BROWN

SUTTON PUBLISHING

First published in 2001 by
Sutton Publishing Limited · Phoenix Mill
Thrupp · Stroud · Gloucestershire · GL5 2BU

Some of the material in this book first appeared in
Edward Bear Esq, 1996.

British Library Cataloguing in Publication Data
A catalogue record for the book is available from the British
Library.

ISBN 0 7509 2814 X

Frontispiece: Benjamin, Hope and Helen Brandreth, playing with
an early American teddy bear in their garden in Bournemouth,
c. 1911. It was probably sent to the children from New York by
their American grandparents.

Typeset in 11/17 pt Photina.
Typesetting and origination by
Sutton Publishing Limited.
Printed and bound in England by
J.H. Haynes & Co. Ltd, Sparkford.

Contents

Preface

Like many people who developed an interest in teddy bears in adult life I do not recall owning a teddy bear as a child. The first teddy bear I remember is a rather charming fellow, since lost, who was given me on my twenty-first birthday by a couple of enterprising friends called Geoff and Jim.

My next teddy bear was bought some time after my children were born and had been given teddy bears of their own. This teddy, a charming, straw-stuffed British bear dating from about 1920 (which I christened with my initials, M.K.K. Bear) is still a favourite today. She has pride of place in The Teddy Bear Museum, Stratford-upon-Avon, which my husband and I opened in 1988 to house our ever-growing collection of bears.

We had never intended a small hobby – buying the occasional elderly and interesting bear – to develop into a feature of Stratford. It just crept up on us quite unplanned, like so many of the best experiences in life. We both loved to go to Stratford to see the RSC perform Shakespeare's plays in Shakespeare's home town. Eventually we bought a small house there so that we could take the children with us at weekends. This brought it home to us that much of what Stratford had to offer at the time (things are very different now of course) did not hold a great deal of interest for children. This led us to think that a teddy bear museum, where we could display our own expanding collection of early teddy bears, might be a possibility. It would be a place where children of all ages, including the grown-up ones, could come and share the pleasure of these fascinating old toys.

The dream came nearer to reality when we found that 19 Greenhill Street, the home of watchmakers and jewellers Archer and Coote, was up for sale. Situated in the heart of Stratford, this beautiful old building, which is a Tudor beamed house behind an Edwardian façade, had all the makings of a fairytale house just right for its furry occupants. The uniqueness of the home we had found for our bears was even more apparent when we later discovered that the house had once been the property of that larger than life monarch Henry VIII. To emphasise its magical atmosphere, the house was decorated with teddy bear *trompe-l'oeil* scenes by a team of people under the direction of artist Sarah Tisdall.

All was finally ready just in time for our official opening by the American Ambassador on 4 July 1988. We felt this was a particularly auspicious day since the teddy bear takes its name from the twenty-sixth President of the USA, Theodore 'Teddy' Roosevelt. By a happy coincidence we discovered that President Roosevelt was himself no stranger to Stratford, having visited the town in 1909. Stratford is therefore bound up with the history of the teddy bear, from its earliest years to the present day.

This small book is packed with information about the history and success of the teddy bear's first hundred years. A success that is all the more remarkable because it saw the rise of an unashamedly old-fashioned toy during the century that witnessed the most rapid technological change the world has ever known. The book tells the story of how the teddy bear developed out of an ongoing fascination with bears, an interest that stretches back for centuries and is found in many cultures. It tells the intriguing tale behind the name, which undoubtedly contributed so much to the teddy bear's rapid celebrity and it traces the steps by which this remarkably popular toy evolved almost simultaneously on both sides of the Atlantic. It looks at the many reasons why the teddy bear became so popular so rapidly and why it has remained a firm favourite with both adults and children. Here too are the real human stories behind such classics of teddy bear literature as Winnie-the-Pooh and Rupert. As the very earliest teddy bears stand on the threshold of officially becoming antiques the book also contains essential and occasionally surprising details about the different makes and types of bears, together with useful hints to help potential collectors of teddy bears and their ephemera.

In just one hundred years the teddy bear has evolved from a mere toy into an icon and for enthusiasts the centenary of the teddy bear is an event to celebrate. For all those enthusiasts and for people who are only just discovering the charms of teddy bears, I hope that this little book will serve as a celebration, a guide and an inspiration to delve deeper into a fascinating and satisfying area of collecting.

Acknowledgements and Picture Credits

I should like to express my great appreciation to the following: Sylvia Coote, manager of The Teddy Bear Museum, Stratford-upon-Avon, who organises everything so beautifully; the staff – Debbie Bunn, Rachel Course, Sheila Barton, Gillian Houghton and Val Perry – for all their hard work and good humour; Ray Coote, for all his help; Neil Miller of Dean's; Oliver Holmes of Merrythought; Clive Dickinson, for his invaluable help with research; and my editors Jaqueline Mitchell and Alison Flowers.

All images included here are supplied by The Teddy Bear Museum, Stratford-upon-Avon, unless otherwise stated. The line drawings and p. 2 of the colour plates are from Seymour Eaton's *The Roosevelt Bears Abroad*, illustrated by R.K. Culver and published by Edward Stern & Co. Inc. of Philadelphia in 1907. In addition, I am grateful to the following organisations for permission to reproduce images:

Christie's Images Ltd, 2001 © – pp. 2, 4, 9, 33 (top), 54, 60, 72, 120; p. 4 (top) of the colour plates

The colour plates are between pp. 80 and 81.

Teddy Bear Chronology

1834   Robert Southey writes *Goldilocks and the Three Bears.*

1894   German toy company Gebrüder Süssenguth shows a
stuffed bear toy in its catalogue.

1897   Bear skittles and 'roly-poly' toy bears feature in the
Steiff catalogue and the Steiff company takes its own
stand at the Leipzig Toy Fair.

1899   Margarete Steiff registers patents for twenty-three of
her soft-toy designs, including a dancing bear and a
bear handler with a brown bear.

1902   *November.* Morris Michtom sells the first 'Teddy's Bear'
in his Brooklyn shop.

1903   *March.* The Steiff company sells 3,000 of its Bear 55PB
to the USA.

1906   *May.* First advertisement for plush bear toys, still called
Bruins, in the American toy trade magazine *Playthings.*
November. First advertisement using the words 'teddy
bear' by American manufacturer E.J. Horsman, in the
American toy trade magazine *Playthings.*

1907   Dean's Rag Book Company publishes *Teddy Bear* by
Alice Scott, illustrated by Sybil Scott Paley. Seymour
Eaton publishes *The Roosevelt Bears* newspaper strip in
book form (USA). Music of the famous song 'The Teddy
Bear's Picnic' is written by American composer
J.W. Bratton. It was originally called 'The Teddy Bear

Two-Step'. 'Little Johnny and the Teddy Bears', first teddy bear comic strip, published in *Judge* magazine. Thomas Edison & Co. (USA) make the first moving picture featuring teddy bears.

1908   Dean's Rag Book Company advertises cut-out and sew teddy bears in *Home Chat* magazine. Large plush bear, unidentified, appears in a Dean's advertisement. The J.K. Farnell company makes the first British teddy bears.

1909   First animated teddy bear cartoon, *Little Johnny and the Teddy Bears*, made in the USA, based on the 1907 comic strip. Death of Margarete Steiff, aged sixty-one.

1910   'The Bruin Boys' first appearance in Arthur Mee's *Children's Encyclopaedia*.

1912   Steiff creates black teddy bears, which are apparently given as mourning gifts following the sinking of the *Titanic*.

1915   Dean's Rag Book Company advertises plush teddy bears, made in its new workshop, in its Kuddlemee toys catalogue.

1919   First non-stop Atlantic flight by teddy bears when aviation pioneers Alcock and Brown take teddy bear mascots with them on record-breaking flight. First British comic-strip teddy bear character, Bobby Bear, published in the *Daily Herald*.

1920   First Rupert Bear picture story, *Little Lost Bear*, written and illustrated by Mary Tourtel, appears in the UK newspaper the *Daily Express*.

1921   German company Schuco patents the Yes/No Bear. J.K. Farnell sets up the Alpha works, making bears designed by Cybil Kent.

1924   First colour animation film with a teddy bear theme made when Walt Disney produces *Alice and the Three Bears*.

1926	First edition of *Winnie-the-Pooh* by A.A. Milne is published.
1930	First teddy bears made by UK firm Merrythought with designs by Florence Atwood. Lyrics of 'The Teddy Bear's Picnic' written by Jimmy Kennedy and set to the original music written in 1907.
1938	HM Queen Elizabeth (now the Queen Mother) grants a Royal Warrant to British teddy bear makers Chad Valley.
1944	Smokey Bear adopted as the mascot of the United States Forest Fire Prevention Campaign.
1952	First appearance of Sooty, the teddy bear glove puppet and magician, on British television.
1953	Steiff celebrates the golden jubilee of Steiff bears with a new style bear, 'a comical young bear cub' called Jackie Baby.
1954	Wendy Boston, Welsh toy-maker, produces the first truly washable teddy bear.
1958	Publication of the first Paddington story, *A Bear Called Paddington*, by Michael Bond.
1959	Walt Disney acquires the rights to Winnie-the-Pooh.
1962	Colonel Bob Henderson launches The Teddy Bear Club. Margaret Baker publishes *The Shoe Shop Bears*.
1969	Peter Bull publishes *Bear With Me* (USA *The Teddy Bear Book*). Jim Ownby launches the charity Good Bears of the World.
1975	Walt Disney's first animated film of Winnie-the-Pooh appears.
1979	Peter Bull designs his traditionally styled Bully Bears for House of Nisbet. Marquis of Bath organises the Great Teddy Bear Rally at Longleat.
1981	Peter Bull's 1907 American bear Delicatessen stars in the television adaptation of Evelyn Waugh's novel *Brideshead Revisited*.

1985 Christie's of London holds the first ever teddy bear only auction. Teddy Bear Artists Guild founded in the USA. Good Bears of the World designate this year as International Year of the Teddy Bear.

1986 World's first teddy bear museum opens in Berlin.

1988 Gyles and Michèle Brandreth found The Teddy Bear Museum in William Shakespeare's home town of Stratford-upon-Avon.

1989 First British Teddy Bear Festival held in London. Happy Anniversary, a 1926 tipped mohair Steiff bear, is sold at auction in London for £55,000 to American Paul Volpp as a forty-second wedding anniversary gift for his wife Rosemary.

1990 First Steiff UK Limited Edition. Hermann Teddy Original seventy-fifth Anniversary Limited Edition. Merrythought Diamond Jubilee Limited Edition.

1994 Teddy Girl, a 1904 cinnamon Steiff bear formerly owned by Colonel Bob Henderson, is sold at auction in London for £110,000 to Yoshihiro Sekiguchi, founder of the Teddy Bear Museum in Izu, Japan.

1996 Teddy Edward, the world's most travelled bear, is bought at auction by Yoshihiro Sekiguchi of the Izu Teddy Bear Museum for £34,500.

1998 Guinness (8.5 mm tall), made by Lynn Lumb of Halifax, England, enters *The Guinness Book of Records* as the world's smallest teddy bear.

2002/3 Centenary of the Teddy Bear celebrated worldwide.

ONE

Life Before Teddy

Distinguished Ancestors of the Teddy Bear

The teddy bear, worldwide symbol of childhood, security, warmth and innocence, has an eternal quality, which makes us feel it has been with us always. In reality, this cuddly stuffed toy, beloved of children and adults alike, was invented in the earliest years of the twentieth century. Yet it seems to have been a part of the childhood landscape for much longer, so that, for teddy bear *cognoscenti*, it has become something of a game to spot the anachronistic use of teddy bears as part of the set dressing of pre-twentieth-century nursery scenes on both the large and small screen.

Teddy bears have achieved their iconic status in a mere hundred years and many people are surprised to find that, despite their quintessentially nostalgic quality, they are more modern than the motor car, the telephone or electric

Two typical nineteenth-century carved wooden hat stands from Germany. Each shows a mother bear reaching for her naughty bear cubs, which have climbed up out of reach.

light. Although now such a popular item with collectors, even the oldest teddy bears cannot, strictly speaking, be considered true antiques until they achieve their first century in 2002. Sadly there are no truly authentic examples of those very first magical 1902 bears in existence.

The soft-toy teddy bear may be a comparative youngster, but bears have been objects of fascination since earliest times. It would appear from cave paintings that bears were both hunted and venerated as far back as 40,000 years ago. This is partly explained by the fact that when bears walk on their hind legs they take on a remarkably human aspect. This resemblance is emphasised further by their faces, which have smallish noses, and their eyes, which look out directly in front, just as they do in human beings.

Where bears roamed wild, they were a powerful part of local myth and folklore, which usually acknowledged some mystical relationship between man and beast. In different parts of the world they were given names that reflected their closeness to the human beings who both feared and admired them. These names included Fur Man, Black Beast and The Strong One. Bears featured heavily in native North American culture, where they were viewed as gods or relatives and sometimes given a family name, such as Grandfather to indicate wisdom.

Bears seem to disappear in the winter when they hibernate. This phenomenon, of apparently vanishing and then miraculously reappearing in the springtime, led to many mythical stories in different parts of the world. For example, in Siberia the bears were said to be messengers who brought word from the spirit world when they reappeared in the warmer weather. The bear's ability to survive the winter without sustenance was sometimes explained by the myth that it could nourish itself by sucking on its own paws. Another legend had it that a bear cub was born as a shapeless form which was literally 'licked into shape' by its mother. As late as the eighteenth century, the poet Alexander Pope wrote:

A rare Staffordshire jug in the form of a chained bear.

A simple hand-carved wooden toy made in Russia in the early twentieth century. Similar toys have been created for hundreds of years.

> So watchful Bruin forms, with plastic care,
> Each growing lump, and brings it to a bear.

The expression 'to lick something, or someone, into shape' – to get it in good working order – has become a part of our everyday language.

For many centuries there was a healthy respect for bears and a desire to pay tribute to these powerful, furry beasts. Naming some of the brightest stars in the sky after them is an example. Early astronomers in India gave the Sanskrit word meaning bright (*rakhi*) to two of the main constellations. But when the ancient Greeks heard this name it sounded to them like their own word for bear (*arctos*), so they assumed the name of the constellations was The Bear. The Romans in their turn then looked for a justification for

The modern coat of arms of Warwickshire incorporates the symbol of the medieval Earls of Warwick – the Bear with Ragged Staff.

the names, which in Latin are *Ursa Major* (The Great Bear) and *Ursa Minor* (The Little Bear). The ingenious story in Roman mythology, which was devised to explain both the origin and names of the constellations, is as follows. Callisto, one of the nymphs of Diana, goddess of the hunt, had two sons by Jupiter, chief of the gods. Juno, Jupiter's jealous wife, changed the boys into bears in an act of spite. Unable to turn them back into children again, Jupiter outwitted Juno by giving his two sons eternal life as bright stars in the heavens.

Bears featured on many medieval coats of arms, including that of the mighty English Earl of Warwick. To this day the county of Warwickshire is symbolised by the bear. The Swiss town of Berne also has a bear on its coat of arms and its name is popularly supposed to come from the German word for a bear. In addition, the bear was the internationally recognised symbol of the powerful Russian Empire right up until the twentieth century.

The power of bears made them inevitable targets for man's desire to prove his superiority over them, not just by hunting them as a source of food and warm clothing but by taming them and reducing them to objects of mockery and entertainment. Bear-baiting, the taunting and mauling of a tethered bear by hounds, was considered fine sport, although many were repelled by it. The diarist John Evelyn, writing in 1670 of a reluctant visit with some friends to the Bear Garden, described the goings on there as 'these butcherly sports or rather barberous cruelties' and expressed himself 'most heartily weary of the rude & dirty passetime'.

With so much interest in them it is hardly surprising that, long before the teddy bear arrived on the scene, bears were represented in many different ways and materials, including wood, metal and stone. Native Americans carved them on totem poles, painted them on masks and gave small, carved bears to their children. Wooden toys, like the popular pull-along bears on wheels, were also found in many Northern European countries, where they have been carved for at least the last thousand years during the long, dark winter evenings when time lay heavy on people's hands. These bear toys tended to be called by their own national pet names. The usual English name for a toy bear was Bruin, while the traditional Russian children's toy, a simple carved wooden bear, was generally called Mishka.

In Central and Eastern Europe bear images were not simply reserved for children's toys but were found on a variety of artefacts and furniture. Woodcuts of bears, particularly tame or dancing ones, were popular in Russia. In nineteenth-century Germany it was fashionable to own a carved hat and umbrella stand in the form of a tree, with a bear cub balancing on the top branch and its mother waiting anxiously below.

From about 1880 mechanical toys called automata, grew in popularity in England, France and Germany. These came in many guises, usually as different types of doll. Sometimes, however, they took the form of dancing bears, which were still a common sight at that time in fairs and market-places throughout Europe, and which are still found in some Eastern European and Asian countries to this day. As well as dancing bears there were drinking bears, which poured wine from a flagon into a cup, and smoking bears. It is unlikely that these were ever intended as toys for

Two Meissen models of young bears playing.

children. Their clockwork mechanisms were far too delicate and expensive to allow children to play with them. And though some of the animals were made of real fur or fur fabric, they invited admiration rather than uninhibited affection and handling. As well as being far from cuddly to the touch they had realistic faces, often with tongues and ferocious fangs. They were clearly aimed at adult collectors, who admired them for their fine workmanship and their novelty value. Today they are greatly valued antiques, which fetch high prices in the auction houses.

BEAUTY AND THE BEAST

The story of Beauty and the Beast, where the beast is usually pictured as a great bear, was first written down by the French writer Madame le Prince de Beaumont in 1763. It was immediately popular and was quickly translated and adapted into other languages. This English version was published in 1843. The extract below, where Beauty has gone to the Beast's palace to fulfil her father's promise, shows how the Beast, despite his animal-like appearance, is endowed with all the best qualities of a princely human being:

Long before the first day had passed, she had felt with all its force the solitude of the place. She quite welcomed the magic flute, and the sounds –

> 'The Beast is near,
> And asks leave to appear!'

and was really glad to answer, 'Appear, Beast!' She shuddered as he approached, but her fear wore off as the Beast stayed conversing with her. When the clock sounded ten he bid her a respectful 'Good night.' The next day she got more used to the place, and even looked out for the time when the magic flute should sound. When the Beast appeared this evening, she looked calmly at his ugliness. She was more than ever pleased with his conversation, which was delightfully witty, wise too, and gentle. Day after day thus passed, the Beast appearing every evening. His visit became the object of the day, and had he been uglier than he really was, I have no doubt Beauty would have ceased to regard it. Thus the time passed for more than half a year: when one evening, after Beauty and the

Beast had been conversing most pleasantly, Beast stopped in his talk and took her hand. Beauty thrilled, but it was not with delight; he had never done so before. Beauty quietly withdrew her hand, at which the Beast sighed deeply, and suddenly he bid her 'adieu!' Some days after this, the Beast again took Beauty's hand, and she suffered it to remain. The Beast then said, 'Beauty, will you marry me?' 'Impossible!' replied Beauty. The Beast groaned deeply, and left as if he felt the greatest grief. The next night no Beast appeared. Beauty listened anxiously for the sounds of the flute, but none were heard. The evening seemed to her the dullest which she had passed since her arrival in the palace. The next evening came, and still no Beast. 'What can this mean?' thought she, 'is the Beast never to appear again! I would sooner have his presence with all his ugliness a thousand times more, than this constant absence.' She had scarcely acknowledged the thought to herself, before the flute sounded and Beast entered. He looked melancholy and pensive, except when Beauty was talking to him. At the usual hour he departed. As he was leaving, Beauty said, 'I hope Beast, you will come to-morrow.' 'It is a great balm to my unhappiness, Beauty, to hear that my visit is not absolutely disagreeable to you.' The Beast continued his evening visits as before, but he never again mentioned the subject of marriage, nor took Beauty's hand. He was as kind and agreeable as ever, but oftentimes Beauty thought he seemed very sad: she feared to ask him the cause. She asked herself over and over again, 'Can I marry him?' and then the thoughts of his excessive hideousness rushed into her mind, and she reluctantly answered, 'No.'

Felix Summerley, 1843

This polar bear is a fur-covered automaton which pours wine from a pewter flagon into a pewter goblet. The liquid is circulated through a rubber tube that runs down the bear's back and along its arm. It was made by the French firm Descamps, which produced similar models from 1866, the year it was founded, until 1935. This particular example was probably made in about 1930.

Bear images featured strongly in literature well before the twentieth century. In *Beauty and the Beast*, Madame le Prince de Beaumont's fairy tale, written in 1740 and swiftly translated from the original French into a number of other languages, the beast eventually turns back into a handsome prince, underlining once again the closeness between bears and human beings. In *Goldilocks and the Three Bears*, published by the poet Robert Southey in 1837, the bears live a human style of life but nevertheless they are not the adorable and harmless teddy bears we associate with childhood today. Goldilocks, the little girl who wanders into their cottage by mistake, is far too frightened of them to stay when she wakes up and discovers they have returned home from their walk.

As well as the classic fairy tales, other less well-known stories featuring bears were written prior to the arrival of the first teddy bear. A good example is *Adventures of a Bear;*

The fairytale of *Goldilocks and the Three Bears* is one of the first pieces of literature in which bears are given human attributes: they sit on chairs, they sleep in beds, they smoke, they eat porridge and they shave before going downstairs in the morning. The English poet Robert Southey first came up with the idea of three bears living a human life together in his collection of writings called *The Doctor*, published in 1837. The idea immediately caught people's imaginations and spawned many versions before it became crystallised as the version we know today of a little golden-haired girl coming across the bears' house in the woods. The popularity of the story helped to pave the way for the concept of the teddy bear which is, in effect, half-bear and half-baby.

This verse version by George Nicol was published in the same year as Southey's story and contains all the elements of the fairy tale as we know it today, except for one: the beautiful golden-haired girl – Goldilocks – is actually an old crone!

The Three Bears

Three Bears, once on a time,
    did dwell
  Snug in a house together,
Which was their own, and
    suited well
  By keeping out the weather.

'Twas seated in a shady wood,
    In which they daily walk'd,
And afterwards, as in the
    mood,
    They smok'd and read, or
    talk'd.

One of them was a great huge
    Bear,
  And one of a middle size,
The other a little, small, wee
    Bear,
  With small, red twinkling
    eyes.

These Bears, each had a
    porridge-pot,
  From which they used to
    feed;
The great huge Bear's own
    porridge-pot
  Was very large indeed.

A pot of a middle-size the Bear
  Of a middle-size had got,
And so the little, small, wee
    Bear,
  A little, small, wee pot.

A chair there was for every
    Bear,
  When they might choose to
    sit;
The huge Bear had a great
    huge chair,
  And filled it every bit.

The middle Bear a chair had he
  Of a middle-size and neat;
The Bear so little, small, and
    wee
  A little, small, wee seat.

They, also, each one had a bed
  To sleep upon at night:
The huge Bear's was a great,
    huge bed,
  In length, and width, and
    height.

The middle Bear laid down his
    head
  On a bed of middle-size;
The wee Bear on a small, wee
    bed
  Did nightly close his eyes. . . .

In this early version the bears'
cheeky visitor was a little old
woman, but the tale still follows
the familiar path.

But she was impudent and bold,
  And cared for none a pin;
So quickly of a spoon laid hold
  The porridge to dip in.

And first out of the great
    Bear's pot
  The porridge she did taste,
Which proving to be very hot
  She spat it out in haste.

She burn'd her mouth, at
    which half mad
  She said a naughty word;
A naughty word it was and bad,
  As ever could be heard.

The middle Bear's she tasted
next,
Which being rather cold,
She disappointed was, and vext,
And with bad words did
scold.

But now to where the small,
wee Bear
Had left his small, wee cup
She came, and soon the
porridge there
By her was eaten up. . . .

She tried the chairs, she tried the
beds, then she fell asleep on the
baby bear's bed.

She slept, as if it had been night,
This sad, old, lazy thing.

The three Bears in their jackets
rough
Now came in from the wood,
Thinking their porridge long
enough
To cool itself had stood.

'Somebody has at my
porridge been!'
The huge Bear's gruff voice
cried;
For there the spoon was
sticking in,
Which he left at the side.

'Somebody has at my
porridge been!'
Then said the middle Bear,
For also in his pot was seen
The spoon, which made him
stare.

These spoons are wooden
spoons, not made
Of silver, else full soon
This wicked Dame would, I'm
afraid,
Have pocketed each spoon.

The small Bear's small voice
said, as in
He peer'd to his wee cup,
'Somebody has at my porridge
been,
And eaten it all up!' . . .

The other Bears look'd at the
bed,
And on the pillow-case
They saw her little dirty
head
And little ugly face. . . .

But when the small, wee Bear
did speak,
She started up in bed,
His voice it was so shrill, the
squeak
Shot through her
ugly head.

She rubb'd her eyes, and when
she saw
The three Bears at her side,
She sprang full quick upon the
floor –
And then with hop and stride

She to the open window flew,
Which these good tidy Bears
Wide open every morning
threw,
When shaved they went
down stairs.

She leapt out with a sudden
bound,
And whether in her fall
She broke her neck upon the
ground,
Or was not hurt at all,

Or whether to the wood she fled
And 'mongst the trees was
lost,
Or found a path which
straightway led
To where the highways
cross'd,

And there was by the Beadle
caught
And taken into jail –
This sad old woman good for
naught! –
Remains an untold tale.

George Nicol (1837)
(after Robert Southey's
version in *The
Doctor* (1837))

and a Great Bear Too by Alfred Elwes, which was published
in London in 1857.

Over thousands of years bears undoubtedly established a
secure place in human culture. Yet as the twentieth
century opened what many consider to be the bear's finest
hour was still to come.

TWO

Teddy's Bear

Origins of the American Teddy Bear

Over the centuries the bear had established a niche for itself in folklore and literature as a fascinating but not particularly friendly figure. How did it turn its reputation upside down and become the universal symbol of love and childhood? How did the new toy with the friendly image acquire its name? And how did it conquer the world?

A teddy bear is fundamentally different from the image of a real bear because it is in no way threatening. The vulnerable appearance of babies brings out the protective nature of adults and it is the baby-like qualities of the teddy bear that distinguish it from the bears that went before. Its face is unrealistically wide, more like the smiling round face of a baby. It has a cute little nose, bright round eyes and a compact, soft body with movable arms and legs, which make it easy to cuddle. As with a baby, in comfort-

SHIRLEY TEMPLE AND TEDDY BEAR

Shirley Temple (born in 1928) was a phenomenally successful child star during the heyday of Hollywood in the 1930s, when she appeared in films such as *Curly Top* (1935) and *Dimples* (1936). She began her movie career at the age of three-and-a-half and her appeal was undeniably sentimental. Here she is seen cuddling a teddy bear in a scene from the 1934 film *Now and Forever* with another Hollywood superstar, Carole Lombard (1908–42).

ing it we feel comforted and in loving it we feel loved in return. But unlike a baby it makes no annoying demands on us; it does not cry or dribble or wake us up at night! An adult responds to a teddy bear because it brings out the adult's protective instincts, but a child responds to it because it recognises another child like itself. In the eyes of its owner, large or small, the teddy bear is dependable, trustworthy, loyal and in no way troublesome.

In the last hundred years the teddy bear has developed along many different paths. The earliest teddy bears, particularly those which were made in Germany, bore a strong resemblance to their wild cousins. Today the word teddy bear can be applied to a wide variety of soft stuffed toys made in a brightly coloured fabric, dressed in fantastical costumes and possibly even sprouting a set of fairy wings. Strangely it is adults who seem to be most drawn to these unlikely and imaginative variations on the teddy bear theme – variations that purists would scarcely recognise as bears at all. This is possibly because adults are 'programmed' to nurture young and helpless creatures and are therefore subconsciously attracted to those soft toys that are most babyish. On the other hand a small child has not reached the stage where it wishes to look after others and

Theodore 'Teddy' Roosevelt (1858–1919), President of the United States 1901–9.

so responds better to a toy which is just that – a relatively realistic version of a clearly recognisable animal.

Being a bear, and not a human-style doll, the teddy bear has the added advantage of not being so obviously a 'girl's' toy. Even the most manly little boys a hundred years ago, when gender stereotyping was encouraged rather than challenged, felt able to be seen with a bear without loss of face in front of their companions. Their fathers felt none of the anxiety they would have experienced had their sons been seen playing with dolls. Yet the teddy was fulfilling the doll's function of being a loving and lovable plaything, to be cared for by its owner and to provide comfort in return. The late Poet Laureate Sir John Betjeman refers in several poems to his teddy bear Archibald Ormsby-Gore, who clearly fulfilled the role of comforter in a rather loveless childhood.

My teddy bear was the very first masculine love of my life.

Barbara Cartland, romantic novelist

. . . Archibald, my safe old bear,
Whose woollen eyes looked sad or glad at me,
Whose ample forehead I could wet with tears,
Whose half-moon ears received my confidence,
Who made me laugh, who never let me down . . .

Michael Bond, creator of Paddington Bear, thinks another reason that bears are in some ways more satisfying than dolls is because, 'With dolls, you know they are only

Clifford Berryman's *Washington Post* cartoon of Teddy Roosevelt's hunting trip entitled 'Drawing the line in Mississippi', which was published on 16 November 1902.

thinking about what to wear, but you never know what a bear is thinking.' Loved by girls and boys, adults and children, men and women, ultimately the teddy's unique appeal when it first saw the light of day was, as it is now, the fact that it acknowledges no boundaries of age, sex or nationality.

Germany and the USA both claim to have invented the teddy bear, but the truth seems to be that it evolved almost simultaneously on both sides of the Atlantic over the winter of 1902–3 in one of those strange coincidences that seem to materialise from nowhere. Since then it has flourished equally in the Old World and the New. Interestingly, although the USA supplied the name, which was such a key factor in the teddy bear's unprecedented penetration of the market, it was the German teddy bear manufacturers who succeeded in exploiting

An Ideal bear, c. 1907. This bear, which belonged to one of the Roosevelt children, is sometimes wrongly assumed to be the original bear made by Morris Michtom. It was donated to the Smithsonian Institution in 1964 by one of President Roosevelt's grandchildren.

their product most widely during this first phase. Indeed, their major market was the USA itself, which could not keep pace with domestic demand.

One reason we tend to acknowledge the American claim to have created the teddy bear is that the very earliest soft-fabric bears from Germany retained their rather intimidating 'real' bear face. By contrast the earliest plush bears made in the USA were very definitely appealing teddy bears, with their broad faces and deceptively human characteristics. The other reason for favouring the American claim is in the origin of the name, which is, without question, American.

We know for certain that in the closing days of 1902 a Russian immigrant called Morris Michtom, who owned a confectionery and stationery shop in Brooklyn, New York, displayed a plush, stuffed toy bear cub in his window and called it 'Teddy's Bear'. We know that this bear took its name from the twenty-sixth President of the USA, Theodore 'Teddy' Roosevelt (1858–1919).

President Roosevelt was a popular man and very aware of his image, which is why he liked to be seen as a rugged, hunting, shooting and fishing type. This was not simply a cynical appeal to the American voter, who had a sentimental attachment to everything that celebrated the pioneering origins of the great nation. President Roosevelt was truly a man of many parts, and hunting was just one of the areas in which he excelled. He had transformed himself, by self-discipline and strength of will, from a sickly, asthmatic child to the epitome of the all-American sporting hero. He was a brilliant natural history scholar and an early environmentalist, who spent time as a rancher in Dakota. It was his forward-thinking idea to conserve vast areas of untouched land as the country's national parks. These parks, such as Yosemite, remain as a lasting monument to him today, as does the Panama Canal, which was built as a result of his initiative. As a soldier he organised and commanded a voluntary cavalry regiment known as 'Roosevelt's Roughriders' during the Spanish-American War. As a politician he built up the strength of the American navy and robustly tackled both corruption in the civil service and corporate monopoly in big business. For his diplomacy in the Russo-Japanese War he was awarded the Nobel Peace Prize. He would, therefore, undoubtedly be surprised, and possibly not totally pleased, to know that the majority of people in the world who remember his name today recall it for something that played only a small part in his extra-ordinary life – the teddy bear.

Some bears have greatness thrust upon them.

Brian Sibley (collector of Winnie-the-Pooh memorabilia)

The story of how the teddy bear came to be named after this remarkable man is a charming one. On 14 November 1902 President Roosevelt was on a hunting expedition in Smedes County, Mississippi. He was there to conduct some tricky political business about the boundary line between Louisiana and Mississippi and the bear hunt had been arranged to afford him a little relaxation. On that particular day the hunting party had had little success and the President had not bagged a single bear. Anxious to put matters right, some of the hunters chased and stunned a 235-lb black bear and tethered it to a tree to give the President an easy target. But when Roosevelt arrived on the scene he declined to shoot a captive animal and declared stoutly, 'Spare the bear!'.

This evidence of sporting fair play was speedily relayed to the world by the *Washington Post*, where a report appeared saying, 'President called after the beast had been lassoed, but he refused to make an un-sportsman-like shot.' Accompanying the report was a drawing by political cartoonist Clifford K. Berryman, in which the large black bear was portrayed as an enchanting bear cub with round eyes and large ears. The cartoon was given the caption 'Drawing the Line in Mississippi', cleverly tying in the President's action with his political reason for being in the state.

Sadly, it seems that despite the President's refusal someone else shot the bear, but this was never allowed to interfere with the public relations potential of the story.

By this time Morris Michtom's wife Rose was already making soft toys for sale. Being Russian immigrants the family was very bear-aware and would have been naturally drawn to the story of the President and the bear. Inspired by the newspaper story, Rose made a jointed, soft-fabric bear toy with the cuddly appeal of a small bear cub. Morris put it in the shop window as 'Teddy's Bear' alongside a copy of the cartoon. It sold immediately, and the Michtoms quickly found they could sell as many bears as they could make.

The story then goes that Morris Michtom sent a letter, with a sample toy bear, to the White House, asking permission to call his bear 'Teddy's Bear'. Michtom later claimed to have received a hand-written note in which the President graciously gave permission, while modestly protesting that he didn't know that his name would be worth a great deal. Since originals have never been produced of either of these letters it is most likely that, while the Michtoms undoubtedly came up with the name 'Teddy's Bear', the story of the correspondence was simply

a clever marketing idea dreamed up in retrospect. Interestingly, to his family Theodore Roosevelt was never known as 'Teddy', but as 'Teedie', his childhood pet name.

A Roosevelt-owned bear, now in the Smithsonian Institution in Washington, is sometimes thought to be the original bear made by the Michtoms for the President. His longish muzzle clearly marks him out as an early model, and he was most probably made by the Michtoms' company a few years later, in about 1907. This bear was indeed once owned by the Roosevelt family for it was the childhood bear of one Roosevelt's grandsons and was donated to the Smithsonian Institution in 1964 by President Roosevelt's great-grandson.

President Roosevelt was not a sentimental man and, as his daughter Alice later revealed, he never cared for teddy bears very much. But the President in the White House found the publicity just as useful as Mr and Mrs Michtom did in their tiny Brooklyn shop. As the popularity of 'Teddy's Bear' soared, President 'Teddy' Roosevelt adopted it as his political mascot, using it first during the 1904 Presidential election campaign. Teddy bears appeared on all sorts of election literature, including menus for fund-raising dinners. Supporters of Roosevelt wore enamel teddy bear pins in their lapels. Roosevelt was also undoubtedly helped by the fact that Berryman used the bear in most of his later political cartoons about the President. Original examples of early campaign mascots can be seen at the Roosevelt Birthplace Museum in New York. After Roosevelt's re-election it is said that small teddy bears, dressed in the uniform of Roosevelt's Roughriders, were placed on the tables at his inauguration dinner in 1905.

Others also appreciated the extraordinary power of the teddy bear symbol and tried to compete with it by taking other animals as their campaign mascots. Although William Taft succeeded as President when Roosevelt stepped down in 1909, Taft's chosen symbol, the possum, enjoyed only brief popularity as a soft toy and was swiftly seen off by the teddy bear.

Sales of 'Teddy's Bear' boomed throughout 1903 and Butler Brothers, one of the USA's largest toy wholesalers, agreed to guarantee the Michtoms' credit with the factory that produced the expensive mohair fabric they needed to make the toys. With Butler Brothers backing them the Michtoms' business was able to expand rapidly. By the end of 1903, Morris Michtom had set up the Ideal Novelty and Toy Company (known as the Ideal Toy Company from 1938). This firm, whose early motto was 'When we do it, we do it right', had factories not only in the USA but eventually also in Canada, Australia and even Japan. It remained a family business until 1982 and closed completely in 1984. When Morris Michtom died newspaper obituaries hailed him as 'The Father of the Teddy Bear'.

For the first year or two of teddy bear production, the toy trade referred to all the new-style toys as 'jointed plush bears' or sometimes 'Bruins', the traditional English name for a toy bear. But because of President Roosevelt's energetic re-election campaign in 1904, the name 'teddy bear' (the 's' was soon dropped) gradually gained ground as a general term for all soft bear toys. After that there was no question of their being called by any other name.

The first use of the name 'teddy bear' appeared in print in November 1906. American manufacturer E.J. Horsman, an early rival of Morris Michtom and his Ideal Toy Company, placed an advertisement in *Playthings*, the trade magazine for toy companies, offering car sidelamps in the form of teddy bears. This novelty ingeniously brought together two of the most fashionable items of the period – motor cars and teddy bears – in an unlikely combination. In the following month Horsman took another advertisement in *Playthings* to promote both 'Imported Teddy Bears' and 'Domestic Teddy Bears'.

In Britain the first recorded use of the name teddy bear occured on 14 September 1907, when the *Daily Chronicle* reported: 'While Europe is sending aloft the diabolo [another toy craze of the time] America is playing with bears . . . The sudden delight in these mere things of the toy shop is due to their name – Teddy-bears.' It is interesting to note from this that, as the teddy bear phenomenon was gathering pace, the toys' popularity was seen by contemporaries to be largely a result of their attractive and evocative name.

For the rest of the first decade of the twentieth century a phenomenal craze for teddy bears swept through the USA, with the inevitable result that certain conservative elements in society started to denounce them as anti-social. Some critics even went so far as to say that it would reduce the national birth rate, as they feared American

Westminster Gazette.]

John Bull and his real Teddy Bear

A cartoon from the *Westminster Gazette* showing the relationship between Great Britain and the USA in the early years of the twentieth century, and depicting President Roosevelt as a teddy bear.

mothers would transfer their maternal instincts to their teddy bears instead of nurturing a new generation of American citizens.

Although Morris Michtom had the distinct advantage of being first in the field with the new toys and of being responsible for the teddy bear's worldwide name, it was not long before many other American toy companies jumped on the bandwagon to take advantage of the soaring popularity of stuffed toy bears. Early American bear manufacturers included the Aetna Toy Animal Company, Hecla, the Bruin Manufacturing Company (BMC), the Harman Manufacturing Company, Gund Bears (which still makes bears today) and, in the 1920s and 1930s, the Character Toy and Novelty Company and the Knicker-bocker Toy Company Inc.

Bears made by these companies in the first years of the twentieth century are highly sought-after collectibles today. Unlike the German manufacturers (Steiff in particular), the Americans were less alert to the importance of maintaining the integrity of their own brands and trademarks. Before the 1920s American bears were not given distinctive, integral tags and buttons or paw labels. Understandably the fragile paper labels they came with were quickly removed, damaged or destroyed. This makes it difficult to make accurate identifications so many years later, unless there is a documented history of the individual bear's provenance.

Many of the early American companies made bears that looked almost exactly the same. For example, several manufacturers, including Ideal and the Knickerbocker Toy Company, made 'googly-eyed' bears (presumed to be based on the wide-eyed bear cub of Berryman's original cartoon) where the black centre of the eye is clearly surrounded by a circle of white, giving a very different look to the more usual black boot-button eyes of the period.

SPEED ACE DONALD CAMPBELL AND HIS BEAR

Donald Campbell (1921–67) pictured with his wife and a member of his support team in 1964, shortly after he had broken the world land speed record at Lake Eyre salt flats in Australia. They are holding his lucky mascot, a Merrythought bear called Mr Woppit (later renamed Mr Whoppit), which had been given to him by his engineer Peter Barker in 1957. Mr Woppit was with Campbell when he

was killed attempting to break the world water speed record on Lake Coniston. The bear floated to the surface and was recovered. Donald Campbell's daughter Gina kept Mr Woppit as her own mascot while later attempting to break a series of women's speed records.

Nevertheless, some of the bears made at this time were so extraordinary and distinctive that there can be no doubt as to their origin. One of the most amusing designs is the Laughing Roosevelt Bear, made by the Columbia Teddy Bear Company in honour of President 'Teddy' Roosevelt, who had very noticeable, large teeth. This bear came in a variety of sizes and fabrics but is always recognisable today as a Columbia Teddy Bear Company bear because it has an open, red-painted mouth, containing either two or four strong white glass teeth. When the stomach is squeezed the mouth opens to reveal the presidential teeth in all their glory.

'Electric-eye' teddy bears were another very recognisable line. The special feature of all these bears is that their eyes are miniature light bulbs connected to a battery placed inside the body. When the mechanism is activated, by pressing either the bear's stomach or a small button on the head, the eyes light up. Several companies made these bears but the best known and most easily identifiable are those produced by the American-Made Stuffed Toy Company of New York. The company began manufacturing them in a variety of colours, including red, in 1907. In 1917, when the USA entered the First World War, American-Made produced a variation on the same theme called National Bears, or Patriotic Bears. The unusual eye-lighting mechanism remained the same but the bears were made with blue heads and red and white bodies, to reflect the American flag.

Another bear where the origin is clear from the mechanism is the 'self-whistling' bear. These bears were made by the Strauss Manufacturing Company from 1907. Recognisable by its distinctive red nose, a 'self-whistling' bear contains a tube with a weight inside. This slides up and down when the bear is inverted to create a whistling sound – an intriguing variation on the more usual 'growler' mechanism.

Many early American bears, particularly those of the 1920s and 1930s, were made with arms and legs that are very thin in order to economise on the amount of fabric and stuffing required. These bears are a far cry from the beautiful hand-made and finished bears that started the teddy bear craze in the first years of the twentieth century and it is rarely possible to be certain which company made them. They represent a new phase of the teddy bear's development. By the end of the First

A typical early American teddy bear, probably an Ideal Toy Company bear, with tubby body, long straight limbs and triangular head. This is the bear being cuddled by one of the Brandreth children in the photograph on p. ii.

World War in 1918, teddy bears had become totally accepted as a childhood 'must-have'. They were no longer the latest craze but were set to become a toy classic. This meant that large manufacturers were ready to move in and exploit the market with cheaper, mass-produced varieties. Paradoxically these cheap American mass-market bears, which earned the name 'stick bears' because of their thin arms and legs, have become a desirable collectible in their own right. This is because, being of poorer quality, they rarely survived in good condition and it is the scarcity of good-quality stick bears that pushes up the price.

Over the next fifty years or so, American bears were produced in many variations. Highly collectible are the American mechanical bears made from about 1907 and the dressed bears – soldiers, sailors and, a particular American favourite, bellhops – which were popular right from the early years. In the 1930s and 1940s in America, as elsewhere, bears were manufactured in modern synthetic fabrics (rayon and nylon) as well as in traditional, but very expensive, mohair plush which is made from the wool of Angora goats.

Despite the infinite variations that make it such an exciting collectible, the early American bear retained its individuality and identity. Of course there are similarities with the early German bears. And naturally technical changes in manufacturing methods and materials, such as the general substitution of glass eyes for the original boot-button eyes after the First World War, occurred at about the same time on both sides of the Atlantic. But put a classic American bear – an Ideal or an Aetna – next to a classic German bear – a Steiff or a Hermann – and you will generally observe at least some of the following differences: American bears have broad, flattish, triangular heads, usually with shorter muzzles than the traditional German bears; ears are rounder and lower-set on the 'corners' of their triangular-shaped heads; their bodies are slimmer and noticeably longer, with shorter and straighter arms and legs; and their feet are round or oval and not elongated like their European counterparts. Early Ideal bears had rather pointed toes, which, along with their triangular heads, help to make identification easier. The naturalistic hump, so much a feature of the Steiff bears, is only found in the very earliest American bears. It is quite clear that, whichever came first, the American and German branches of the teddy bear family evolved quite separately and they continue to evolve in their own styles today.

THREE

Bärle and Friends

Origins of the German Teddy Bear

Germany owes its claim to be the original birthplace of the teddy bear to the long-established toy company Steiff, which is based in the small town of Giengen an der Brenz in Swabia. Although Germany had been the main European centre of the toy trade for many years, Steiff was not founded as a toy company. It was begun as a mail-order clothing company by an extraordinary woman called Margarete Steiff.

Margarete was born in 1847 and as a child she contracted polio, which left her confined to a wheelchair for the rest of her life. Despite this, and at a time when it was far harder for a woman to achieve independence than it is today, she was determined to remain self-sufficient and to use her skills as a needle-woman to earn a living. At first she worked as a dress-maker, usually going to other people's houses to make the clothes for the entire house-

Margarete Steiff at her factory in Giengen. She is seen, on the right, sitting at a work table in her wheelchair.

hold. From this, capitalising on the expansion of the newly established postal service, she branched into mail order. This was a novel and very successful idea and by dint of hard work she rapidly expanded her one-woman business and began to employ other people, although still working from her parents' home.

Much of the clothing Margarete Steiff sold was made of a warm red felt and the company was called the Felt Mail Order Company. Rather than waste the material that was left over when the main patterns were cut out, thrifty Margarete bought a commercial pattern for an elephant-shaped pincushion which she then had made up from the felt scraps. These novelty pincushions were offered as an

Margarete Steiff.

extra in the catalogue. To her surprise the pincushions were a run-away success and it became clear that people were buying them to give as children's toys. Always quick to identify a commercial opportunity, Margarete Steiff began to offer felt toys in all sorts of different animal shapes and to adapt some of them as pull-along toys on metal wheels. After a few years the toys had completely outstripped the clothes as the factory's main output. Fritz Steiff, Margarete's brother, joined the company and began to look for ways of making the toy business grow. In 1889 the business moved out of the Steiff family home into a building with its own shop outlet attached and in 1893 the company name was changed to the Felt Toy Company.

Well-run and commercially aware, Margarete Steiff's company grew rapidly, and so did its product range. In 1897, under the direction of Richard, one of Fritz's children, the company exhibited independently, with its own stand, at the prestigious Leipzig Toy Fair. Its catalogue showed lots of stuffed animals, including camels, giraffes, sheep, cows, dogs, cats, rabbits, horses and kangaroos, to name but a few. It certainly also produced a number of toy bears at this time, among them a set of skittle bears (which are much sought after by collectors today) and a pull-along polar bear on wheels, both of which were featured in the same 1897 catalogue. There were also various 'dancing' bears standing on their hind legs and fixed either to rotating discs or to 'roly-poly' platforms.

In 1899 Steiff patented patterns for twenty-three of its stuffed animals, including a polar bear, a dancing bear and a bear with a handler. These patents form part of the basis of the Steiff claim to have invented the teddy bear. However, these early bears were very realistic, they were not jointed, and they were very hard and stiff. They had

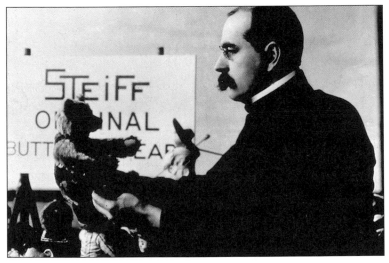

Richard Steiff with one of his very earliest teddy bear designs.

not developed the baby faces and cuddly qualities that characterise a true teddy bear but were more like fur-covered versions of the wood or metal automata being made at the time.

The Steiff Company was very much a family affair. As well as Margarete Steiff's brother, Fritz, who was her main adviser, all six of Fritz's sons eventually worked for the company. Foremost among these was Richard, who had studied at art school in Stuttgart and specialised in the design of the soft-toy animals, basing many of them on the real-life ones he had sketched at Stuttgart zoo. In Europe, unlike the USA, dancing bears were still a feature of street entertainment, and these too were an inspiration for Richard Steiff's ideas. Basing the designs directly on real, living bears helped to give early German bears a more naturalistic look than their American counterparts.

At the very beginning of the twentieth century Richard Steiff designed a toy bear which was coded Bear 55PB. It was realistic in manner, with claws, a pronounced hump and a true bear's sharp-nosed face, but it had several of the characteristics that came to be associated with the teddy bear. It was made of soft plush (the P in the code) and it was jointed (the B in the code) so that its arms and legs were movable. The 55 referred to its height in centimetres.

At the beginning of 1903, only a very short time after the Michtoms first displayed their stuffed plush bear cub, a shipment of 55PB bears was taken to New York by Paul

EARL MOUNTBATTEN OF BURMA AND HIS BEAR

Louis Mountbatten (1900–79), who grew up to be first sea lord, photographed in a sailor suit with his teddy bear, *c.* 1904. The teddy bear was a novelty and very fashionable so early in the twentieth century. Louis Mountbatten was a great-grandson of Queen Victoria and his family name was originally Battenberg. Presumably this Steiff bear was sent to him by one of his many German relatives.

Steiff, another of Margarete's nephews. To everyone's disappointment the new Steiff bears were initially unsuccessful in the USA. Paul's view was that, as well as being too expensive, they were too large and heavy to have the cuddly child-appeal necessary for a successful toy and which we now recognise as the essential characteristic of the teddy bear.

However, at the Leipzig Toy Fair in March 1903, only a few months later, the Steiff Company reached a major turning point in its history with the selfsame bear! Ironically, the man who brought this about was an American, Hermann Berg, the buyer for George Borgfeldt and Co., a famous New York department store. The story goes that, disappointed to have found nothing special or innovative at Leipzig, and on the point of leaving, Berg paid a last-minute visit to the Steiff stand. The sample products were already being packed away, but when Berg said he was looking for a new cuddly toy for young children, Richard Steiff searched out the sample of his new bear. Hermann Berg loved it, placed a massive Christmas order for 3,000 bears, and by doing so established a permanent place for himself in the history of the teddy bear.

Sadly, there are no surviving examples of this very first Steiff jointed bear, not even in Steiff's own museum, although there is a slightly blurred photograph of a stout, realistic-looking bear, with large feet and curved paws, in a

1903–4 Steiff catalogue. Richard Steiff accurately judged the needs of the market and, despite the huge order for this first jointed bear, decided he needed to develop the design further rather than resting on his laurels.

The realistic style was rapidly transformed to a less authentic, but infinitely more appealing, baby-faced toy with boot-button eyes, and

A Steiff wide-eared bear, 1904–5, one of Richard Steiff's experimental designs.

soft, clawless pads. The new style, which appeared in the 1904–5 catalogue under the name Bärle, was coded 35PB. Very few of these original bears or their even rarer small brothers, coded 28PB, exist today, so they are much prized by collectors.

By mid-1905, Bärle had evolved still further into an even less naturalistic and more doll-like teddy bear, with a noticeably softer filling, although the characteristic curved front paws remained, as did the long feet and narrow ankles. The pads were still made of felt and the eyes were still made of boot buttons but instead of a realistic black nose made of hard sealing wax the nose on the new bear was stitched in thread. Gradually the hump on the back became a little less prominent and the long muzzle was shortened to give a broader, less-threatening face. The new

version also came in a much wider range of sizes, including a 45-inch bear the size of a child. By 1910 their were fourteen sizes of Steiff bears available.

During the experimental period of 1904–5, as the company was finding its classic style, the Steiff family tried out a number of variations on the original pattern. One of these was the wide-ear design, where the ears are set on the side of the head. These wide-eared bears were made in beige or white and the nose stitching was beige, giving an overall lighter look. Although this design was not ultimately successful, wide-eared bears still appear regularly at auction, where they are quickly snapped up by collectors and dealers.

In 1907 alone Steiff made a phenomenal 974,000 of its classic bears and the period from 1903–8 later became known as the 'Bärenjahre' – 'the Bear Years' – in company mythology. In 1906 the company changed its name for the third and last time to Margarete Steiff GmbH, reflecting the fact that the founder's name was by now recognised as a guarantee of the quality of its toys and, in particular, of the teddy bears that made up the most important part of its output.

Sales began to build in Europe and Britain but the USA, despite a mini-recession in 1907, remained far and away the biggest customer. By now the USA had became unashamedly 'Teddy Bear Mad'. Inevitably the German name Bärle bowed to market forces and from 1906 Steiff bears were marketed as teddy bears like their American counterparts.

An amusing little anecdote was concocted in retrospect to give the Steiff account of how the teddy bear came by its name, in an attempt to reconcile the German claim to be first to create the teddy bear with the fact that it undeniably sports the name of an American president. Alice Roosevelt, the President's daughter, celebrated her marriage in 1906 with a grand party at the White House. The caterer, anxious to create memorable and attractive table decorations, made a last-minute decision to buy up dozens of small Steiff bears. The little bears were then dressed as sportsmen – hunters with rifles and fishermen with fishing rods – as a graceful compliment to the bride's father and his sporting pastimes. During the meal the President was asked what type of bears they were and when he pronounced himself baffled a guest stepped in to explain that they were all 'Teddy's Bears'. This explanation lends a fairy-tale air to the Steiff company's sensible commercial decision to adopt the definitive American name for its own bears.

Some sixty years later the English actor and pioneering bear collector Peter Bull visited Alice Roosevelt. This forthright lady (her best-known quotation is 'If you haven't anything good to say about anyone come and sit by me.') stated quite categorically that teddy bears had been totally absent from her wedding festivities. Despite her

A giant Steiff bear, about 4 ft tall, made in the early 1920s. Very few of these bears were made. A similar bear was bought by the psychic Uri Geller in 1996 for £11,500.

flat denial the story persists to this day as part of the fast-growing archive of teddy bear myth and legend. Whether the account is true or not, we know that Bärle irrevocably changed his name to Teddy to exploit the craze gripping the USA.

So, by a curious trick of fate, Morris Michtom's Ideal bear and Richard Steiff's Bärle seem to have been created at almost exactly the same time in 1902–3 and between them established the traditional teddy bear style we all know and love today. With the decisive standardisation of the name this first stage in the life and times of the teddy bear, on both sides of the Atlantic, was complete.

FOUR

'Button in Ear'

German Teddy Bears Conquer the World

Steiff was the first European company to make true teddy bears. Since then, despite the rapid proliferation of competitors, it has retained its leading position by good design, careful attention to quality and ferocious defence of its designs and innovations.

Germany was the foremost toy-making country in the world at the end of the nineteenth century and it is hardly surprising that there were plenty of very competent toy firms eager to jump on the bandwagon of the teddy bear's extraordinary popularity. From the 1890s Steiff had begun patenting its designs in an effort to gain some legal protection for its products. In this it showed great prescience at a time when people were much less careful about safeguarding their intellectual property than they are now. As well as patenting its designs and technical innovations (there is a pattern registration for a jointed plush bear dating from as early as July 1903), the company also devised clearly identifiable trademarks to protect its products.

While most toy-makers continued to identify their toys with disposable paper hang tags, Steiff devised its famous 'Button in Ear' trademark, which ensured that all the company's toys were clearly and permanently distinguishable from those of its competitors. In 1904, as the teddy bear market was escalating and Steiff's competitors were blatantly copying its designs, Franz, another of Margarete Steiff's nephews, came up with the idea of

A hug of early Steiff bears made between 1903 and 1906. Left to right: a classic early Steiff, a wide-eared bear, a metal-rod bear and a centre-seam bear.

putting a small blank metal button into the left ear of each Steiff soft toy. Since a simple blank button was not considered sufficiently distinctive in law the actual words 'Knopf im Ohr' ('Button in Ear') were also registered as a trademark in 1905.

Over the years, while the trademark words have remained the same, the buttons have been designed in different ways. The very first buttons were blank. From the end of 1904 and throughout 1905 they were stamped with the Steiff emblem of an elephant, a reminder of the felt elephant pincushions on which the company's fortune was founded. Later buttons carried the name Steiff in various scripts. These buttons are a useful indicator of the exact age of the toy. Steiff has defended its logo and the identifying button with great ferocity. Any firm that tried to put an identifying button, or a metal tag of any kind, in the left ear of its bear, was taken to court. As a result the button has become synonymous with Steiff and even when it has been lost a small distinct hole in the left ear is generally regarded as a sufficient indication that the toy was made by Steiff.

As another way of outwitting the many competing bear-making factories that sprang up all over Germany and which were copying Steiff designs, Margarete and her nephew Richard constantly experimented with creating new variations on their first teddy bear. The method of making movable joints was improved. The very earliest bears of

1903 were made mobile by a simple string (or sometimes wire thread) system which broke easily. Next came an arrangement of metal rods, which is found in some of the experimental bears made in 1904. The joints on these bears, which had black sealing wax noses like the other very earliest bears, moved well but were very heavy – exactly the problem Richard Steiff was trying to avoid. As a result

A rare Steiff metal-rod bear made in 1904. This bear is in excellent condition and still has the original sealing wax nose with realistic nostrils.

very few were made and they are highly prized. Ultimately, in 1905, disc joints made of heavy card and held in place by metal pins were developed. This solution to the problem of maximum mobility and safety was so successful it is still used today.

New fabrics were also introduced. The very earliest bears had been grey, beige or white. Gold mohair plush was introduced and became a hugely popular option. Black bears also enjoyed a vogue although they have never been as consistently popular as the lighter colours. A consignment of 494 black bears was exported to the English market in 1912–13. Tradition, probably fanciful, has it that these black bears were given to families mourning

Alfonzo, the 1908 red Steiff bear made for Princess Xenia Georgievna of Russia. He is seen here without his original cossack costume.

relatives or friends lost when the *Titanic* sank in 1912. Black bears are difficult to make appealing because the dark plush loses the detail. This is particularly important with the eyes, which can get lost against the dark background. To counter this problem Steiff resorted to its old favourite, red felt. A circle of this was placed behind the eyes to form a background from which they would stand out clearly. Where this red felt was not used the bear becomes even more valuable. In 1996 a record price of £24,200 was achieved at auction for an early black Steiff bear. The fortunate owner had bought it earlier in the year at a car-boot sale for £100.

As well as shipping vast quantities of its popular new designs Steiff also took commissions for individual orders. A famous example is the red bear, Alfonzo, made in 1908 for Princess Xenia Georgievna, the four-year-old daughter of George Mikhailovich, the Grand Duke of Russia. This bear was sold in 1989 for £12,100. It fetched this impressive price not only because it is unique but because it has a romantic and well-documented history. An authentic personal story always adds value to a bear, particularly when it includes a princess. When the First World War broke out in 1914, the little Princess Xenia, accompanied by her teddy bear, was visiting her royal relatives in England. She never returned to Russia or saw her adored father again, for he was assassinated after the Bolshevik revolution. Alfonzo remained the Princess's faithful companion and a tangible link with her Imperial family and past until her death in 1965.

To improve the desirability of their bears still further, Steiff fitted them with 'growlers'. The early mechanism was a sort of 'squeeze-box' which had to be pressed to create a sound. In 1908 the automatic 'growler' was first used. This works by tilting the bear back and then forward again and is still used today. Margarete Steiff even tried to get a patent for a tilt 'growler' that growled the word 'teddy', in order to emphasise, yet again, the Steiff company's claim to be the original inventor of the teddy bear.

Margarete Steiff died in 1909. By a remarkable coincidence, this was also the year in which Theodore Roosevelt finished his tenure as President of the USA. After her death, it was left to Margarete Steiff's extensive family to protect their company's interests against increasing competition. Despite all their efforts, it was proving impossible to prevent rivals from making teddy bears. Germany had long been the heart of the toy industry and many German teddy bear companies developed from existing toy factories, while others started up specifically to exploit the new fashion.

Probably the most successful company to prosper alongside Steiff was Hermann, founded after the First World War by Bernard Hermann. He, like Max Hermann, who founded Hermann Spielwaren (Hermann Toys), was the son of Johan Hermann, the owner of a long-

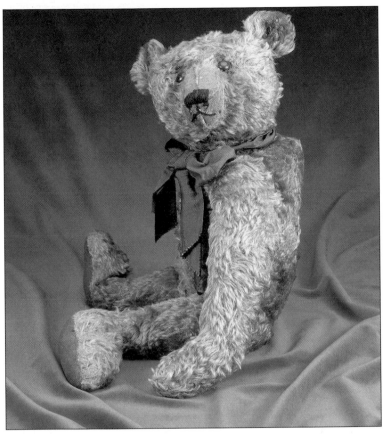

A beautiful 1905 Steiff bear, a particularly collectible example because of its unusual cinnamon-coloured mohair and the centre seam along the snout.

established toy company in Neufang. Bernard Hermann's company flourished under the direction of his three sons who took it over and renamed it Gebrüder Hermann (Hermann Brothers) in 1948. It remains a successful family business to this day.

The Hermann company has always been known for top-quality bears and it, like Steiff, wished to make its bears clearly distinct from inferior imitations. Because Steiff always acted promptly to prevent other companies using the idea of a trademark button, even if it was not attached to the toy's ear, Hermann decided to avoid confrontation and used identifying medallions. These have varied in design over the years but since 1952 they have carried the words 'Hermann Teddy Original'. Hermann bears tend to be slightly 'chunkier' than Steiff bears. They often have a clipped muzzle or a muzzle in different fabric from the rest of the bear. Many Hermann bears have an open mouth (sometimes with tongue), which is unusual outside Germany.

Gebrüder Süssenguth, which was set up in 1894, also manufactured teddy bears with distinctive open mouths. A very early version of their bear Peter has some claim to being the first teddy bear; it appeared well ahead of Steiff's bears. Although the oldest surviving version of this distinctive bear dates from 1925, a very similar bear is illustrated in the first Süssenguth catalogue, printed in 1894, and this predates the Steiff catalogue containing pull-along bear toys by a good three years. Unfortunately, Peter and his nineteenth-century predecessors have a rather frightening appearance, with a realistic open mouth (complete with teeth and fangs set in red gums!), a movable tongue and rolling eyes. These features are quite out of keeping with the appealing friendliness that is so essential for a teddy bear. Peter and his 'forebears' are toy bears but, like the nineteenth-century Steiff bears, in the opinion of most experts neither Peter nor his ferocious-looking ancestors who feature in that early catalogue would qualify as true teddy bears.

Other outstanding German teddy bear manufacturers whose bears are much sought after today include Gebrüder Bing, Schreyer and Company (Schuco) and, during the 1950s, the Koch Company and the Anker Company.

Gebrüder Bing started in 1863 as a company making tin kitchenware. From these beginnings it was a short step to making metal toys, many of them with clockwork mechanisms. In 1907, when the American teddy bear craze was at its height, Bing began making its own plush

A rare Gebrüder Bing clockwork bear, made in about 1910. Note the Bing identifying button on the side seam.

bears. At first an arrow-shaped identity tag was used in the ear. Steiff took Bing to court because it believed Bing's ear tag was too close to its own 'Button in Ear' trademark. As a result the metal ear tag was replaced by a stud (Steiff insisted it must not be called a button) in the bear's side, under the left arm. Steiff was still not appeased and in 1920 Bing started to use a metal label affixed to the bear's right arm.

In fact the Bing bears were not styled like the Steiff bears. The very earliest Bing bears have sweet, rather round faces with small ears, short snouts and round oval feet, not unlike their American counterparts. Later Bing bears, from about 1920, have longer, flat-topped, blunt-ended snouts, usually with shaved muzzles.

Because of its established expertise in making mechanical toys, Bing made many bears with wind-up clock mechanisms. Some of these made the bear's head move from side to side. Another frequently employed mechanism, activated by a wind-up key under the left arm, causes the bear to move backwards and forwards supported on a stick attached to his right arm. Meanwhile, the arm on the left swings backwards and forwards. As well as being used for a number of dressed walking bears this mechanism lent itself to other actions including skating and skiing, with the bears dressed in a variety of different and appropriate costumes.

One of Bing's most popular designs was a tumbling acrobat bear, which was suspended by two chains and which swung up and over a cross bar. Another was the tumbling bear. This works by turning the overlong arms round to wind up the mechanism. When it is set down the bear tips forward onto its extended arms which then unwind, causing a series of somersaults. Both of these actions were very similar to Steiff designs and helped to compound the bad feeling that already existed between the two companies. In 1910 Steiff took Bing took court saying that the company had breached the patent for the Steiff Purzel-Bar, which also swung up and over a cross bar.

The Bing Company went bankrupt in 1932 during the worldwide economic slump, so its bears are now comparatively rare and highly collectible, especially if the wind-up mechanisms are still working and/or they are wearing the original felt clothes.

Schreyer and Company was founded in 1912 by Heinrich Schreyer and Heinrich Müller. Müller had worked for Bing and so Schreyer and Company built on this expertise to specialise in mechanical toys. In 1921 Müller, with his new partner Adolph Kahn, registered the trademark Schuco. This was the year that Schuco introduced their famous 'bellhop' design. The bear is styled like an American hotel bellhop, complete with a perky pill-box hat and a leather shoulder bag. Its head and paws are of mohair but the body is made of a suit of felt clothes – a red jacket and black trousers.

The Yes/No Bear, a teddy bear classic, was patented by Schuco in 1921. Bears with a Yes/No mechanism have heads that can turn from left to right or move up and down. This mechanism is operated by using the tail as a handle. After the Second World War the mechanism of the Yes/No bears was modified and they were given the new name of Tricky bears. Yes/No and Tricky bears were produced in a variety of sizes and styles from 1921 until the 1970s, when Schuco was bought out by Dundee Combex Marx.

Schuco is also famous for the wide range of delightful and innovative miniature bears which it began making in 1924. Many of these were made of metal covered in mohair, a reminder that the company had started out manufacturing tin toys. The tiniest of these miniatures, known as Piccolo bears, were initially intended as promotional giveaways but proved

An early Schuco Yes/No bear. The stubby little tail, which works the head-turning mechanism, is clearly visible.

so popular they became a range in their own right. Schuco miniatures, including Piccolo bears, were made in many colours, including green, red and mauve, as well as the more usual golden shades of mohair. These bears are typically 3.5 in (9 cm) tall, although the Piccolo bears were as small as 2.25 in (6 cm). Those made in the 1920s, and later in the 1950s, even had felt pads on the ends of their tiny limbs, but in the 1930s Schuco miniature bears were made without defined paws.

As well as traditional-style miniature bears, Schuco also designed and produced miniature mechanical bears,

An electrically driven Schuco automaton made in 1935. The bear's head moves from side to side to read the paper while the monkey nods.

including tumbling bears and bears in little motor cars. Miniature novelty bears were very popular for the adult market. They were sold as brooches or opened up to reveal mirrors, powder compacts, perfume bottles and lipstick cases or even small pots of jam. Schuco miniatures have become extremely popular with collectors.

In 1936 Germany's political climate led Schreyer and Company to cease trading. It started up again after the war with an American branch importing products from the

German factory. Despite initial success, Schuco, like many traditional and long-established European firms, could not compete against cheaply produced mechanical toys from the Far East and the company finally went bankrupt in 1972.

The First World War, which had indirectly boosted the domestic toy industry in Britain and the USA had been devastating to the German toy industry. Even when the war ended shortages meant that bears were made from materials other than traditional high-quality mohair. For a few years German manufacturers, including Steiff, used an inferior material called paper-plush, but this was very fragile and few examples exist today.

However, by the mid-1920s German manufacturers were back on course and bears were made in a greater variety of styles than ever before. The teddy bear's face became even less realistic as German teddy bears moved closer in appearance to their American cousins. German bears of the 1920s and 1930s have much sweeter, baby-like faces than most pre-1918 examples. Although all gener-alisations have their exceptions when identifying and dating teddy bears, one fairly typical feature of this gener-ation of bears is that they have glass eyes rather than the black boot buttons of the earlier toys.

The mohair plush used to make the bears between the wars tended to be very long and luxuriously silky. Bing in particular liked to make its bears with high-quality fabrics, which is why Bing bears survive in such excellent condition today. Pastel-coloured mohairs became fashionable, particularly yellow, baby pink and baby blue. A greater variety of materials, including cotton plush, was used. Also originating from this time, and still popular today, is two-toned 'tipped' mohair, which gives the fur a delightful textured and natural effect. A famous example is a bear called Happy Anniversary, a 1926 Steiff in brown tipped mohair. Happy was brought by American collector Paul Volpp in 1989 as a wedding anniversary present for his wife Rosemary. It cost what was then the highest price ever paid for a teddy bear, £55,000.

Ribbons and bows became a standard adornment to give the bears extra appeal. Dressed bears, which had been popular before 1914, were in vogue again and bears were produced wearing dresses, sailor suits and soldiers' uniforms. Bing specialised in dressed bears. The idea of clothing bears was taken a step further with many firms producing teddy bear accessories such as tiny bear-sized suitcases, pyjamas, hair-brushes, spectacles, parasols and umbrellas. These innovations did a great deal to re-establish German bears in the all-important American market-place.

German teddy bears, like their American and British counterparts, developed and changed rapidly throughout the 1950s, 1960s and 1970s. There was a trend away from the purely traditional style. This was partly due to

SIR JOHN BETJEMAN AND HIS TEDDY BEAR

Sir John Betjeman (1906–84) photographed with his beloved Steiff bear, Archibald, in about 1910. Sir John, created Poet Laureate in 1972, had derived great comfort from his bear during a rather bleak Edwardian childhood and often celebrated Archie in his poetry. When he died Archie was in his arms.

inevitable variations in fashion after half a century of making the same product. But there were also other, more practical reasons. Steiff, Hermann and other German manufacturers (as well as rival American and British companies) had been forced by wartime restrictions and technological advances to make bears in fabrics such as rayon and sheepskin as well as natural mohair. The demand for greater hygiene meant that bears were not always filled with traditional kapok or wood-wool but were stuffed with foam, polyester or similar machine-washable materials.

Change was also triggered by competition from cheap, mass-produced bears from the Far East, where there were no qualms about breaking away from the 'rules' that governed the appearance and manufacture of a quality, traditional teddy bear. The established style of German bears was strongly influenced by the new softer style of these rival imported toys, while at the same time they struggled to compete on price. All these factors contributed to the development of a more cuddly type of bear in the post-war years.

Steiff began making bears such as Jackie, a cub design brought out in 1953 to celebrate the fiftieth anniversary of Steiff teddy bears. Jackie had a much rounder face than the classic teddy, the body was short and plump and the legs were also short, with rounder paws than the classic Steiff bears. In the same year Hermann also produced a newly styled bear, with a short body and short arms and legs.

Soft-Bear was another example of Steiff adapting to the new market. This bear had a very soft filling and only its arms were movable. In 1957 Steiff brought out Cosy-Teddy with a soft synthetic filling, again catering for the soft-toy market. One of the most successful Steiff bears from this period was the Zotty (shaggy), which had the traditional German open mouth but the modern-style soft body.

Over a period of sixty years, the German teddy bear had been refined and developed. It had conquered the world, becoming one of the most recognisable icons of the twentieth century. The German teddy bear industry had adapted to change and survived two world wars, remaining pre-eminent in the creation of high-quality authentic teddy bears. Yet during the 1960s it became clear that low-priced, mass-produced bears were not simply affecting the appearance of the new generation of bears, they were beginning to threaten the very existence of the traditional hand-made bears and the toy firms that produced them.

FIVE

Rule Beartannia

The Unique Contribution of the British Teddy

The love affair between the British and the teddy bear goes back to the first decade of the twentieth century when the first Steiff bears were imported from Germany.

Britain is not the only country outside the USA and Germany to have made teddy bears; France, Austria, Holland and Australia are just some of the places that have produced excellent bears. But after the USA and Germany, Britain has done most to advance the teddy bear's fame and popularity, primarily by creating teddy bear characters, like Winnie-the-Pooh and Paddington, which are known and loved throughout the world.

Because of the coincidence of the accession of King Edward VII to the British throne in 1901, and the fact that the King was affectionately known to his subjects as Teddy, it is even sometimes suggested, although wrongly, that the teddy bear was named after the roly-poly British monarch.

THE TEDDY BEARS' PICNIC

The Roosevelt Bears, Teddy B. and Teddy G., enjoying what may have been the first ever teddy bears' picnic with their new friend, King Edward VII.

> They all sat down on rocks near by
> To eat a lunch of deep apple pie
> And English jam and crumpets round
> And nuts and candy, a dozen pound,
>
> And toast and tea and hot-cross buns
> And hard-boiled eggs and sally luns
> And cherries ripe and roasted grouse
> Which the king had ordered from the house.

From *The Roosevelt Bears Abroad*, by Seymour Eaton.

A delightful hug of bears made by the British toy firm J.K. Farnell between 1908 and 1968.

This led to a lot of puns inspired by the King's enthusiasm for beautiful women. One of the many jokes that referred to the King's mistresses made mention of the glamorous actress, Lily Langtry, who was said to prefer her Teddy bare.

The company that claimed to have made the very first British plush teddy bear was the old-established firm of J.K. Farnell. Josef Eisenmann, the sole importer of Steiff bears into Britain before 1910, could not get enough German bears to meet the overwhelming demand, so he persuaded the son and daughter of J.K. Farnell to change their production from fabric-based household goods, such as tablecloths, to soft toys. It is generally accepted that J.K. Farnell began making its first teddy bears in 1908.

Other companies quickly followed Farnell's example, including the British United Toy Manufacturing Company, W.J. Terry (Terryer Toys) and the East London Toy Factory. Unlike the Germans, British firms were not careful about putting labels on their bears when they first began producing them. Bears were definitely being made from about 1908 but no British bears of this period can be positively identified and dated. So, although J.K. Farnell's claim to have been the first is widely accepted, it cannot be proved for certain.

The company that can provide documentary evidence of its early history more accurately, and which also has a good case for being the first to make a British teddy bear, is the Dean's Company, which continues to flourish from its base in South Wales where it relocated in 1972. The original company was Dean and Son, Publishers, based in London. They devised the novel concept of making indestructible cloth books for children – Dean's Patent Rag Books – which

DEAN'S "RAG" KNOCKABOUT TOYS.

HYGIENICALLY STUFFED AND FINISHED.

The Three Bears.

THESE toys have a place of honour in our determined frontal attack on the HIGH COST OF LIVING.

They are just as effective as a fully-dressed plush bear, and at less than a quarter the cost. One is seated, one stands erect, and one on all fours. These poses are not haphazard, but have been carefully copied from those assumed by the living animals. The illustrations give only a general idea of their many good points: the actual toys speak for themselves by the humorous, carefree outlook upon life and its problems, expressed in their jolly faces and breezy attitudes.

They are amusing, lovable, inexpensive: no playbox is complete without a set.

Ref. No D 251.

One Bear **1/9**   Set of Three **5/3**

Supplied to the Trade packed ¼ dozens assorted.

Ref. No. D 251.

Please quote Reference Letter and Number when Ordering.

Cloth teddy bears advertised in an early Dean's catalogue and making the point that they were cheaper than bears made from mohair plush.

became an immediate success with parents and nannies. As the 1920 catalogue so neatly put it, 'To appreciate their numerous advantages, it is only necessary to come into

74

contact with young children who have reached the age when they wear their food and eat their clothes.'

Dean's Rag Book Company quickly added a toy range to its products. Dean's Rag Knockabout Doll and Toy Sheets were cut-out dolls printed onto the same robust fabric as the company's books. What could have been more obvious than to offer rag book stories about teddy bears and a range of 'cut-out-and-sew' teddy bears too? This is exactly what Dean's did. It published a rag book in 1907 entitled *Teddy Bear*, with delightful pictures by Sybil Scott Paley and words by Alice Scott. The story begins:

> Once Dick and Betty pass a shop
> You may be sure they stare
> For staring at them with a smile
> Is Mr Teddy Bear.

In 1908 Dean's placed an advertisement for cut-out-and-sew rag doll teddy bears in the magazine *Home Chat*. 'Mamma' bear and her twin children, 'Teddy' and 'Sissy', either light or dark brown, were offered for the princely sum of 1s (5p) with the assurance that they were 'absolutely British'. A year later, Samuel Finsburgh and Company was advertising a similar cut-out bear made from a sheet of flannelette.

A photograph used in Dean's advertisements from 1907 to 1912 shows a little girl wearing a knee-length apron and dangling a small plush teddy bear in one hand. Although this is the only photographic evidence, a similar bear appears in a drawing of a collection of Dean's toys used to illustrate an advertisement in 1908. It is tempting to think that the plush bear was made in 1907 in the Dean's workshop as one of a kind specially for the advertising photograph, and later drawn as one of the collection of Dean's toys advertised in 1908. If so, it would certainly be the very first British teddy bear, a whole year older than the ones attributed to J.K. Farnell. This is an exciting thought for teddy bear historians, but probably the mystery of who really made the first British bear will never be solved to everyone's satisfaction.

Dean's swift exploitation of the teddy bear craze, and its progression from teddy bear books via cloth teddy bears to fully jointed plush teddy bears was probably in part a result of teddy bear importer Josef Eisenmann joining the board of directors in 1905. Prior to the First World War Britain still imported most of its teddy bears from Germany. In 1912, when the trend reached its height in Britain, it has been estimated that anything up to 2 million bears were sold. Eisenmann would have been eager to encourage more home-grown teddies to satisfy an apparently insatiable demand.

It was the devastating effect of the First World War on the German toy industry that left the field clear for the development of the British firms. Before 1914 British textile mills had been exporting high-quality mohair plush for use by the German teddy bear factories. Now the fabric was bought by the established British teddy bear manufacturers and by newcomers such as the Wholesale Toy Company, the British Doll and Novelty Company and Isaacs and Company.

Dean's formed the British Novelty Works' Productions to make a wide range of soft toys, including plush teddy bears. These early Dean's bears were not marketed as Dean's but sold under the Kuddlemee trademark ('Kuddlemee on Toys has the same significance as the Hallmark on Silver', was the company's bold claim). The 1915 Kuddlemee catalogue has drawings of the first reliably dated British plush teddy bears. Master Bruno and Miss Bruno were dressed plush bears, available in white or gold and in three sizes. Like all the best bears they had 'voices'. Also mentioned, but not pictured, was the British Bear. The first photograph of this magnificent beast is probably in the picture that appeared in the 1916 Kuddlemee catalogue to advertise Dean's sand toys for seaside holidays; in the background of the beach scene, lolling against a rock, is a very typical British teddy bear with a long, stout body, straight arms and legs and flat feet. Another wartime Dean's bear was described as 'The Bear of Russia, Germany's Crusher', a timely reminder that the bear was a traditional symbol of Russia, Britain's ally in the war.

The phase of the teddy bear's history between the two world wars has often been called 'The Golden Age of the Teddy Bear', and this was as true in Britain as it was in Germany and the USA. The outbreak of the First World War in 1914 had marked a turning point in teddy bear history by putting a stop to the German domination of the manufacture of bears and giving teddy bear companies in other countries a chance to catch up. German factories were turned over to war work, raw materials were in short supply and export was impossible. The sudden drying up of German teddy bear supplies during and immediately after the

A highly collectible Dean's Tru-to-Life black bear, designed by Sylvia Wilgoss in the mid-1950s.

First World War, coupled with the fact that Britain was the main source of the quality mohair used in the very best teddy bears, meant that the British toy industry had the opportunity of matching German standards of production and design. As a result, during the 1920s and 1930s, they forged ahead.

A classic Hugmee bear made by the British firm Chiltern. The large feet with velveteen pads are reinforced with card and have five claw stitches. Hugmee bears were made in several sizes from 1923 to the 1960s. This bear has the moulded nose introduced in 1958.

Dean's began producing plush bears under the Dean's name instead of the original Kuddlemee label and the company also introduced its classic A1 bears. J.K. Farnell expanded its successful Alpha line. Farnell's great claim to fame is that the bear purchased in 1921 by Dorothy Milne (known to her family as Daphne) for her son Christopher Robin, and familiar to generations of children as Winnie-the-Pooh, was one of their Alpha bears.

Other famous British teddy bear firms were established in this golden period, often by amalgamating with existing small toy firms. Chiltern Toys was started by Leon Rees and a former J.K. Farnell employee, Harry Stone. They developed the business from a toy company started by Rees's father-in-law, the successful importer Josef Eisenmann, before the First World War. In the 1920s the company was known as H.G. Stone and Company and used the Chiltern trademark. Later it became Chiltern Toys. Hugmee bears, with their broad, floppy heads and short, chunky bodies, proved one of the most perennially successful designs of the Chiltern range and variations were made for over forty years. Chiltern bears are highly collectible, particularly the novelty bears such as those with wind-up musical boxes in their tummies or the Wagmee bears, whose tails are manipulated to make the heads move from side to side rather like the Schuco Yes/No bears.

Chiltern Skater bears like this were made in the 1930s and 1950s.

A typical Edwardian Christmas card, which shows how quickly teddy bears joined dolls as an integral part of the nursery scene.

One of the Roosevelt Bears enjoys a camel ride on a trip to Egypt. From *The Roosevelt Bears Abroad* (published in the USA in 1907). The Roosevelt Bears books were written by Seymour Eaton and illustrated by R.K. Culver.

The cover of *Rupert, Little Bear's Adventures*, written by Mary Tourtel and published in 1925. In these very early collections of stories Rupert is shown with blue checked, not yellow checked, trousers and a blue rather than red jumper.

A nineteenth-century French clockwork automaton in the form of a muzzled bear. This realistic, fierce-looking bear contrasts sharply with later, more cuddly, teddy bears.

This ceramic tile panel by the Pre-Raphaelite artist Sir Edward Burne-Jones illustrates how, in the fairy tale Beauty and the Beast, the beast was typically depicted as a ferocious bear.

A one-off artist's bear, Red Devil, created by pioneer British bear artist Gail Everett. In the 1980s Gail Everett also produced a series of 'Punk' bears with brightly coloured mohican hair styles.

Dracula, by bear artist Gail Everett, created for Hallowe'en 1988 as a companion for Red Devil.

The King and Queen of America, created for the 1990 Kansas City Teddy Bear Jubilee by American bear artists Monty and Joe Sours, of Gladstone, Missouri. The bear artist movement began in the USA in the early 1980s.

Henry VIII Bear, created in a limited edition of 200 by Welsh bear artist Sue Schoen in 1991 to celebrate the 500th anniversary of the birth of King Henry VIII, who once owned the building that houses The Teddy Bear Museum, Stratford-upon-Avon.

Traditionally styled British bears from the 1980s and 1990s in party mood.

Novelty teddy bears have become nearly as popular as the real thing. Here marzipan teddy bears enjoy a 'teddy bears' picnic' on top of a child's birthday cake.

A very early American teddy bear, probably made by the Ideal Toy and Novelty Company in about 1910. Inset: the bear is pictured in 1998 with his original owner, Miss Mattiegrace Sharpe.

A hug of early British bears. Left to right: a typical 'Georgian' bear made between 1920 and 1930, a bear, possibly by J.K. Farnell, made in about 1913, a Dean's mouse-eared bear dating from about 1921 and one of the first Merrythought bears, made in about 1931.

Mary with her little bear behind.

COPYRIGHT 1907.
BY DANFORTH & CO.

Early greetings and postcard manufacturers could not resist the inevitable puns on the word bear, as this cheeky postcard, printed at the height of the teddy bear craze in 1907, demonstrates. The bear behind is a typical Steiff bear of the period.

Chad Valley, a Birmingham-based printing company when it began in the early nineteenth century, progressed from printing children's board games and jigsaw puzzles to making toys and teddy bears. Although dating is difficult, it appears to have begun making bears during the First World War and expanded in the 1920s by amalgamating with a small soft-toy company called Issa. In 1938, Chad Valley received the coveted Royal Warrant from Queen Elizabeth (now the Queen Mother) who bought one of its most popular designs, the lovely, chunky Peacock Bear, for her daughters Princess Elizabeth and Princess Margaret.

Pedigree Toys was created by Lines Brothers in 1937. This firm already made soft toys but the Pedigree label was intended to specialise in teddy bears. Pedigree bears developed their own distinctive look: their faces were fairly flat, with short snouts and distinctive mouth stitching, which curved up on either side to give the bear a smiling expres-

A 1960s Chad Valley bear with the Royal Warrant on his foot.

sion. The earliest Pedigree bears had black plastic noses, the arms and legs were short and straight, the feet were simply round ends to the legs and there were no paws or claws. Pedigree Toys opened a factory in Belfast in 1946 and bears from this period are easily dated as they are

A trio of bears made between the First and Second World Wars.

tagged with the label 'Made in Ireland'. The company also opened factories in other countries, including New Zealand, Australia and South Africa.

The Merrythought Company, which began in 1930, is the epitome of the golden age of teddy bear manufacture. The company has its roots in the Yorkshire textile trade, which had supplied the mohair for the very first German teddy bears. W.G. Holmes (whose grandson runs the present factory) and G.H. Laxton decided to create a soft-toy company that would use the mohair fabric they manufactured at their mill in Yorkshire. They invited A.C. Janisch of J.K. Farnell and C.J. Rendle of Chad Valley to join the new company and bring their expertise. Space was rented in a former iron foundry in Coalbrookdale (now Ironbridge) in Shropshire. Their designer was a deaf mute called Florence Atwood, who was a school friend of Mr Rendle's daughter. She created all the patterns for the firm's early catalogues and remained their chief designer until her death in 1949. Some of her patterns are still in use today.

Merrythought is an old word for a wishbone, so the company's trademark is a wishbone. This is found on a button in the ear of its first bears. Later bears have a label sewn on one of the feet. Early Merrythought bears include Bingie, a cuddly bear cub in tipped brown and white curly plush, the Magnet Bear ('the bear which attracts') and a

LAUGHING BABY BEAR

A new conception of a "toy" bear cub, natural shape, will stand or sit in a chair. An art silk line in golden brown and biscuit or black and white.

No.	Price.	Approx. Height.
S1064/2 ...	10/8 each ...	12½ in.
S1064/3 ...	14/- each ...	15 in.
S1064/4 ...	18/- each ...	18 in.

All our Toys are made of the finest quality materials obtainable.

A page from the 1932 Merrythought catalogue.

range of art-silk plush bears in sophisticated art-deco shades including Eglantine, Azure, Nil, Mimosa, Venus and Clematis, all of them chosen from 'the 1932 selections of the Paris Dress Designers'.

When the Second World War started in 1939 the Merrythought factory was turned over to war work. Production was inevitably affected in all the British toy factories, and even when the war ended, the constraints of rationing restricted what could be made. During the war many people knitted bears for their children using wool recycled from old clothes or made teddies from patterns printed in women's magazines. They were rarely made in quality mohair plush and more often in any spare fabric an owner had available, but many collectors like to buy these unique old bears.

As a result of wartime rationing, bears were made of some interesting and unexpected fabrics by established manufacturers as well. Popular options were sheepskin or a form of cheap plush made from wood-pulp and mohair. From the early 1950s rationing was no longer a consideration but hygiene became important to prospective purchasers. Wendy Boston Playsafe Toys was set up in Wales in 1946. As the name implied, the company specialised in safety. In place of the glass eyes, with their potentially dangerous wire shanks, which had become the norm after about 1920, the company created special plastic eyes with screw locks.

A hug of royal bears belonging to Princess Margaret, Prince Philip, Princess Anne and Lord Frederick Windsor. The large classic Wendy Boston bear belongs to Lady Gabriella Windsor.

Throughout the 1920s, 1930s and 1940s, kapok had been the preferred material for stuffing the bears as it created a softer toy than wood-wool. Kapok did not wash and dry successfully, especially when the bear was made of traditional mohair. Nor did the early types of synthetic foam stuffing. However, a new type of stuffing, made of

Although a lot has been written about other British teddy bear companies the story of Wendy Boston Playsafe Toys has remained obscure. The company was set up in Abergavenny, South Wales, in 1946 by Wendy and her husband Ken Williams. Wendy Boston was the designer and Ken was the marketing genius who contributed equally to the company's success.

Originally from Birmingham, where Wendy had studied design and Ken had been a journalist, the couple moved to Crickhowell, near Abergavenny, after the Second World War. Wendy had begun making soft toys for young friends and relatives. Ken took a batch of these to Cardiff, sold them all for £100 and realised that he and his wife had the abilities to create a thriving company.

Other toy manufacturers had experimented with new washable fabrics and stuffing and were changing over to child-proof eyes, but Wendy Boston Playsafe Toys showed initiative by successfully using these factors in its marketing, including the inspired and reassuring name Playsafe. It was a simple but brilliant idea to make a teddy bear that could be machine-washed and then safely put through the mangle. At trade fairs buyers from the toy stores would flock to the Wendy Boston stand to watch Ken Williams enthusiastically demonstrating how the bears could be squashed between the rollers of the mangle and come out the other side none the worse for wear. As well as washability the bears also boasted unbreakable eyes, which had a safety-locking mechanism at the back to prevent them being removed and swallowed by young children.

Wendy Boston's designs were clever because they took the best of the new toys which were beginning to come in from the Far East – their softness, bright colours, easy-care fabrics and simplicity of manufacture – and combined them with originality of appearance and innovation of design.

Playsafe washable teddy bears had distinctive square heads and large round muzzles. As well as safety eyes and easy care fabrics, the bears had ears which were cut from the material as an integral part of the head, so that the toys could be pinned onto washing lines by their ears. The front and back of the body were cut in one piece so that arms and legs could not be torn off. Although Wendy Boston bears did not have jointed limbs they were clearly 'real' teddy bears and cleverly presented in cellophane-topped boxes, marking them out from their cheaper, mass-produced rivals.

The Playsafe bear, combining Wendy Boston's distinctive design and Ken Williams's very clever trade name and skilful marketing and advertising, convinced parents that the Wendy Boston bear was indeed the safest and most hygienic bear on the market. Ken Williams' flair for publicity was legendary. When the Queen visited Wales he made sure everyone knew she had taken away with her a Wendy Boston Playsafe bear for Princess Anne.

The company flourished for nearly thirty years, reaching its peak in the late 1950s and 1960s, when it accounted for 25 per cent of all British toy exports. This success was even more surprising at a time when the British toy industry was itself being threatened by cheap imports from the Far East. Yet, unlike those other stalwarts of the British teddy bear world, it ultimately failed to survive the threat from foreign imports. Wendy and Ken had no children of their own to carry on the business and after thirty years they wanted to take a back seat. Ironically, the business closed in 1976, without finding a buyer, just as the home-grown teddy bear industry was poised for a revival.

plastic pellets, was used by Wendy Boston when it made the first all-synthetic machine-washable bear with plastic eyes in 1954. Throughout the 1950s and 1960s bears (both home produced and imported) made from nylon fur fabric were popular because of the novelty that they could be machine washed.

Traditional companies like Dean's, Merrythought and Chiltern Toys adapted their styles and made bears in the new wonder fabric Bri-nylon, which came in a variety of bright fabrics as well as the more usual brown and beige. Merrythought included a teddy in its 1958 Jumpee range that was described as 'a washable cuddly bear, with a specially soft foam stuffing and made of super quality silk plush in assorted pastel colours'.

During the 1960s and 1970s, not only the appearance but the very survival of traditional British bears, like their counterparts in the USA and Germany, was threatened by the influx of cheaper soft toys imported from the Far East. Several firms closed down altogether, including J.K. Farnell, which made its last bears in 1968. In 1967 Chiltern Toys was taken over by Chad Valley, which in turn was taken over by Palitoy in 1978; Palitoy was later sold to an American firm. Wendy Boston Playsafe Toys closed in 1976. Pedigree Toys survived for some years in the hands of various different owners, but finally ceased trading completely in 1988.

To combat the competition from abroad those established firms that survived felt pressure to make washability and softness their priorities and to cut corners on the expensive process of making a hand-finished bear. It is perhaps not totally surprising that the traditional appearance of the teddy bear was threatened during the post-war period. For collectors, most of the imported mass-produced bears do not qualify as true teddies and they have no value in the sale rooms (although, of course, they make delightful cuddly toys and give a lot of pleasure to their owners).

By the end of the 1970s only Dean's and Merrythought remained of the early British companies, and the future of the traditional British teddy was very much in the balance.

SIX

Bear Necessities

Teddy Bear Nonsense and Novelties

In just a few short years at the outset of the twentieth century, teddy had made the leap from being a novelty to becoming a necessity for every self-respecting child and for a surprisingly large number of adults. Equally rapidly, everyday items and giftware in teddy bear guise flooded onto the market. What could not be disguised as a teddy bear was covered with teddy bear decoration. In 2001 a company even launched a closed circuit surveillance system for a young child's room where the camera and microphone are concealed in the head of a large teddy bear.

We are inclined to assume that teddy bear novelty items are a phenomenon of the late twentieth-century commercialism, but this is far from the case. Right from the beginning of that century the popularity of the teddy bear was exploited in a wide range of novelty items and memorabilia that we would recognise today, such as key rings, mugs, wine coasters, pens, pencils, book ends and, as the century drew on, fridge magnets.

The fact that the first-known teddy bear advertisement, published in November 1906, was for a teddy bear novelty accessory, not for a toy bear, is the clearest indication that teddy's versatility was immediately recognised.

This first advertisement, using the expression 'teddy bear' (rather than plain 'bear' or 'Bruin'), was placed by E.J. Horsman, who offered side lamps for cars in the form of teddy bears. Horsman did not advertise actual toy teddy bears until December 1906. In addition to teddy bear lamps, teddy bear mascots for car bonnets were also popular in the early years of the twentieth century. In 1913 Steiff devoted a whole page of its catalogue to motor-car accessories, many of which had a teddy bear theme, including 'bear standing on radiator cap' and 'bear climbing up the radiator grille'.

Although it was determined to protect its commercial interests, Steiff was far from purist in interpreting the uses to which teddy bears could be adapted. In addition to all sorts of mechanical bears, musical box bears

A wind-up German bear that plays the violin, made in about 1925.

A German-made, possibly by Steiff, child's muff, which dates from about 1908.

and bears on wheels, it devised totally new uses for its bears. In 1907 it produced a teddy bear with a lace-up middle which concealed a cylindrical metal hot-water bottle. In 1930, a Steiff bear with a body that could fit over a teapot was introduced. It also made pyjama cases and beautiful teddy bear muffs for children. The hot-water bottle containers were not a commercial success, only ninety of them were made between 1907 and 1914, and as a result they are now rare and highly sought after. The muffs, on the other hand, proved a triumph and were copied by many other firms. Versions are still made today, by Steiff itself and by the British firm Merrythought, among others.

Purses were another early novelty item adapted from the bear itself, as opposed to being merely decorated with a teddy bear motif. In the 1980s there was a craze for children's school bags in the form of teddy bears which appeared to be riding on their owners' backs.

Because teddy bears were perceived essentially as children's toys, the teddy bear theme was applied to almost everything made for the nursery. In the USA in particular silver spoon and pusher sets for babies were decorated with teddy bear motifs and given as christening gifts. Other popular christening presents were teething rings or baby rattles with a silver teddy bear attached. Nursery china sets decorated with teddy bears were made by

A purse teddy, c. 1913. Similar purses were made until about 1950.

many manufacturers before the First World War and even tinier sets were made for dolls' houses and teddy bear tea parties. Hermann and Steiff have made lots of versions of these over the last hundred years and they make delightful additions to a teddy bear display as well as being accessories for a dolls' house. Teddy bear money boxes also date back to the first decade of the twentieth century. Because of the association of bears with honey, china honey and jam pots are always popular.

For adults, teddy bear jewellery, in expensive gold or silver or in cheaper costume jewellery versions, was soon available and remains popular today. Jewellery is sold by teddy bear firms like Steiff and Merrythought as well as by jewellery manufacturers. Particularly popular at one time were bracelets with teddy bear good luck charms attached to them. Teddy bear chess sets have been made

from time to time as well as a variety of printed board
games featuring teddy bears. Highly collectible are teddy
bear thimbles, desk items such as inkwells and cigarette

lighters, and dressing table objects like hand mirrors and manicure sets.

In the nineteenth century, cheap printing and photographic reproduction techniques were developed. These technological developments, combined with the introduction of reliable, cheap postal services in the USA, Britain and Europe, led to the phenomenal growth of the greeting card and postcard industries. Early postcards and greeting cards featuring teddy bears are now collectors' items and the teddy bear theme is perennially popular as the current success of Hallmark's sentimental teddy bear themed greetings cards 'Forever Friends' shows. Teddy bear playing cards are another greatly prized collectible.

It would be impossible to keep track of every teddy bear related item devised by ingenious manufacturers. Not only did companies make teddy bear products, they exploited the strong public affection for teddy bears in order to advertise anything from biscuits (Peek Freans) to ladies' stockings (Bear Brand stockings). Today the range of teddy bear products on offer is more overwhelming than ever, and much of it is mass produced. But as well as quantity there is still quality to be had for the discerning bear lover who chooses with care from the new as well as the old.

SEVEN

Celebrating Teddy

An Icon for the Twentieth Century

Since the teddy bear's debut in 1902/3 people have been celebrating teddy in music, in song, in literature and, of course, on stage and screen. It was in 1906–7, at the height of the American teddy bear craze, that the Roosevelt Bears, characters created by Seymour Eaton (the *nom de plume* of writer Paul Piper), illustrated by R.K. Culver, first made their appearance. The books, which began life as a newspaper strip, were verse stories about Teddy G. (good) and Teddy B. (bad), who dressed in suits and looked like American businessmen. They were intended, as Seymour Eaton later wrote, 'to teach children that animals, even bears, may have some measure of human feeling'. The role of teddy bears as a force for good is underlined in the story in which the Roosevelt Bears visit England and meet King Edward VII. As they leave, the King muses:

It would help me carry my country's cares
If every home had Teddy Bears.

'Hurrah! Hurrah!' said TEDDY-B,
'And now for home across the sea;
Back to the land where girls and boys
Keep Teddy Bears for chums and toys;
Across the prairie with its fields of corn,
To the mountain den where we were born.'

Seymour Eaton (Paul Piper),
The Roosevelt Bears Abroad, 1907

Comic-strip character Biffo the Bear makes one of his early appearances on the front page of the *Beano*, 7 February 1948.

As well as the books themselves, and the bears, old and new, which are based on them, people love the Roosevelt Bear collectibles such as postcards, which were part of their great commercial success at the time.

A decade later, another American writer, Thornton W. Burgess, wrote a delightful series of books, the Green Forest Series, which featured Buster Bear, Mother Bear and their twins Boxer and Woof-Woof. Like *The Roosevelt Bears*, these stories were full of plain country wisdom, and the illustrations by Harrison Cady show the bears dressed in human clothing.

Newspaper and comic strips were popular in Britain, just as they were in the USA. As early as 1908, the strip Bobby and the Woolly Bears appeared in the magazine the *Butterfly*. The Bruin Boys were created for Arthur Mee's *Children's Encyclopaedia* in 1910; they also starred in the *Rainbow* comic when it was launched in 1914 and moved to *Tiger Tim's Weekly* in 1920. Equality among the sexes was finally achieved in 1925 when the magazine *Playbox* featured the Bruin Girls, led by Tiger Tim's sister Tiger Tilly. Twenty years later, another star bear, Biffo, made his debut in the *Beano*.

But far and away the most popular bear character to appear in a British newspaper strip was Rupert. Half-bear half-boy, he inhabits a magical world where strange and wonderful things are possible. He was invented in 1920 for the *Daily Express*, as a rival to the successful *Daily Mail* strip character Teddy Tail. Unlike Teddy Tail, who long ago ceased to feature in the *Daily Mail*, Rupert still appears every day in the *Daily Express*.

A Rupert Bear book jacket from a facsimile copy of the 1936 *Rupert Bear Annual.*

Over more than eighty years the style of drawing Rupert Bear has changed and evolved. Mary Tourtel's early creation looked rather like a toddler, with a nappy inside his little checked trousers. Each of the different artists who succeeded her, and the colourists who added magic and depth to the characters and the backgrounds, has brought their own vision to the character. Sometimes he has been drawn with a white face and at other times with a bear's brown face, although the soft toys tend to be made in white fabric.

Rupert is not merely a curiosity bear from the past; he continues to flourish to this day, having starred in his own television series and videos. In 1984 former Beatle Paul McCartney released an award-winning video entitled *Rupert and the Frog Song*. Rupert soft toys and gift items are testimony to his enduring popularity and he has become so much a part of the culture that his face has even appeared on postage stamps. Since 1983 Rupert has had a fan club called the Followers of Rupert, which publishes a magazine called *Nutwood*.

There is no more famous literary bear than Winnie-the-Pooh, whose exploits have been translated into more than twenty languages, including Latin. Societies of Winnie-the-Pooh enthusiasts are to be found all over the world.

Along with his friends Christopher Robin, Piglet, Tigger, Kanga, Roo and Eeyore, Winnie-the-Pooh was created by the English writer Alan Alexander Milne (1882–1956). He based the characters on his only child, the real Christopher Robin, and on Christopher Robin's own collection of cuddly nursery toys.

A.A. Milne was already a successful author and playwright when he published his first children's book in

THE MAKING OF RUPERT

Mary Tourtel (née Caldwell, 1874–1948), the creator of Rupert Bear, came from an artistic family. Her brother was an illustrator of children's books and her father and grandfather designed and cared for much of the stained glass in Canterbury Cathedral. Mary Tourtel herself showed great early promise as an artist. She won an impressive number of medals at art school before going on to illustrate children's books, specialising in drawing animals. An impressive woman who showed great independence in an age when women were not encouraged to have careers, Mary even took up flying and was a pioneer aviatrix.

In 1920 her husband, the poet Herbert Tourtel, was working for the *Daily Express* and knew that the editor of the paper was looking for a children's character to compete with those being created for rival newspapers. Mary's expertise at drawing animals made her the obvious choice. She devised the character of Rupert Bear for her first story, *Little Lost Bear*, and at the very beginning her poet husband helped write the distinctive rhyming stories.

Initially Mary Tourtel alternated the Rupert stories with those of another character, a little girl called Margot. But Rupert was clearly the readers' favourite and eventually Margot became incorporated into the Rupert stories.

After Mary Tourtel's failing eyesight forced her to retire in 1935, a number of artists drew Rupert, the most successful of whom was Alfred Bestall (1892–1986). Bestall was already an established children's illustrator when he took over the Rupert stories. Interestingly he had illustrated books for A.A. Milne, creator of Winnie-the-Pooh, and also for Enid Blyton. Bestall, who introduced some of the best-known additional characters, including Tiger Lily and the Old Professor, drew Rupert and wrote the rhyming stories for thirty years. He retired officially in 1965 – his last story to appear in the *Daily Express* was *Rupert and the Winkybickies*. However, he continued to contribute pieces of artwork up until the age of ninety and his paper-engineering inserts in the Rupert annuals led to his being elected President of the British Origami Society at the ripe old age of eighty-six.

Often overlooked in the history of Rupert Bear is the contribution of artist Alex Cubie (1911–95), Alfred Bestall's assistant, who succeeded him in 1965 and drew Rupert for about ten years. The current Rupert illustrator is John Harrold, whose first Rupert story was published in the *Daily Express* in 1976, and who took over the design of the covers and distinctive endpapers for the annuals in 1978. Harrold continues the tradition of fine artwork that was established by Mary Tourtel. The words are now provided by Ian Robinson.

A delightful Rupert gallery, together with displays on the life and work of Mary Tourtel, can be seen at the Heritage Museum in Mary Tourtel's home town of Canterbury.

> Two jolly bears once lived in a wood,
> Their little son lived there too.
> One day his mother sent him off
> The marketing to do
>
> She wanted honey, fruit and eggs,
> And told him not to stray,
> For many things might happen to
> Small bears who lost the way

The first lines of Mary Tourtel's first Rupert Bear story, which appeared in the *Daily Express*, 8 November 1920

THE QUEEN MOTHER AND TEDDY BEAR GIFT

A charming picture of the Queen Mother (then Duchess of York) on an official visit to East Ham in London in October 1926. She is clutching a teddy bear given to her as a gift to take home for her six-month-old baby daughter Princess Elizabeth, now Queen Elizabeth II.

1924. This collection of verse, written for Christopher Robin and entitled *When We Were Very Young*, brought A.A. Milne almost immediate international fame. Milne's next three children's books – the Winnie-the-

> Three Cheers for Pooh!
> (For Who?)
> For Pooh –
> (Why, what did he do?)
> I thought you knew;
> He saved his friend from a wetting!
>
> A.A. Milne, *Winnie-the-Pooh*, 1926

Pooh classics *Winnie-the-Pooh* (1926), *Now We Are Six* (1927), and *The House at Pooh Corner* (1928) – followed closely behind. From the very first they were hugely successful worldwide, and their popularity has never waned. Today the books, with their spin-off titles and merchandising – everything from Winnie-the-Pooh animated films to duvet covers and yoghurts – are the foundation of a multi-million-pound industry, which grows bigger every year. Milne's son Christopher sold his share of the literary estate. The remaining chief beneficiaries of the Milne estate – the Garrick Club in London where A.A. Milne was a member, Westminster School, which he attended as a boy, and the Royal Literary Fund – receive an estimated minimum of £2 million a year between them.

Despite their extra-ordinary success A.A. Milne was never happy that the four small volumes brought him international acclaim while all the other books and plays, of which he was far more proud, were soon forgotten.

A.A. Milne, the author of the Winnie-the-Pooh stories, pictured with his son Christopher Robin and Christopher Robin's bear, the original Winnie-the-Pooh. The photograph was taken in the mid-1920s when the books were first published.

Nor did the original Christopher Robin, for whom the books were first written, gain much pleasure from them. To him they were a source of unwanted celebrity. He began to resent them and the inescapable shadow they cast over the rest of his life.

Christopher Robin grew into a shy and gentle man who shunned fame and preferred the low-key life of a writer and bookshop-owner in the West of England. He resented the way his name had been exploited, as he saw it, and accused his father of having achieved his international success by 'climbing upon his child's shoulders' and of having 'filched from me my good name and left me with the empty fame of being his son'.

As an adult Christopher Robin was estranged from his parents and gladly divested himself of all claim to the Winnie-the-Pooh copyrights long before their purchase by Disney rocketed the proceeds into the stratosphere – a sad outcome for the sunny little boy who had been Winnie-the-Pooh's loving owner.

A.A. Milne eventually gave the original toy bear to his publisher in the USA. As the bear's fame grew the publishers decided the office was an inappropriate place to keep him and donated him to the New York Public Library, where he is currently kept on display, along with Christopher Robin's other famous toys, in the children's section of a small branch of the library in central Manhattan.

Interestingly the drawings of Pooh do not look like Christopher Robin's own bear. This is because the illustrator of the stories, E.H. Shepard, based his work on a completely different bear, a Steiff called Growler, which belonged to his own children. By a curious coincidence E.H. Shepard's daughter Mary grew up to become the illustrator of another children's classic, *Mary Poppins*. By an even stranger coincidence Mary Poppins's umbrella (or more accurately the umbrella that inspired Mary Poppins's creator P.L. Travers) is also on display in the New York Public Library in the same room as the original Winnie-the-Pooh.

One of the magical aspects of Winnie-the-Pooh is his unusual and unlikely name. Yet Christopher Robin's bear had not always been called Winnie-the-Pooh. That delightful 'hunny' loving, bear of 'little brain' was initially christened Edward Bear. The very first words of the book Winnie-the-Pooh are, rather confusingly: 'Here is Edward Bear, coming downstairs now, bump, bump, bump, on the back of his head, behind Christopher Robin.' After this introduction he is referred to by his more famous name, and no reason for the sudden change is offered to the reader.

This selfsame Edward Bear that later achieved fame as Winnie-the-Pooh, was bought from Harrods' department store in London in 1921 by Alan and Daphne Milne as a first birthday present for their baby son. He was a lovely, silky Farnell bear with a chunky body, long curved arms, a shaved muzzle and glass eyes. At first he was referred to simply as 'Bear'. As the baby grew into a little boy the bear was given the quite conventional name of Edward. But when Christopher Robin grew more independent he changed his bear's name just once more to a title of his own choosing, and a teddy bear legend was born.

The Milnes often took their son on outings to London Zoo. A particular attraction at the zoo at that time was a large Canadian brown bear called Winnie. Winnie had been bought as a cub in 1914 by a young Canadian army vet called Harry Colebourn, who paid $20 for her. He named her Winnie after his home town of Winnipeg. The bear cub became an army mascot and was brought across to

England with the regiment when Canada entered the First World War. When Colebourn was sent to serve in France Winnie was placed in London Zoo for safe-keeping, where she lived until her death in 1934. Nowadays there is a small museum in her memory in the town of White River, Ontario, where Harry Colebourn bought the bear cub. Each year the small town hosts a teddy bear festival to honour Winnie the brown bear and the world famous toy to which she unwittingly lent her name.

Having admired the real, live bear in the zoo, Christopher Robin began to use the name Winnie for his own bear. He then coupled it with the name Pooh. Pooh was the title given by the Milne family to the pet swan they used to feed on a river near Arundel in Sussex. Cotchford Farm, the Milne's country house, was in the Ashdown Forest in Sussex. This idyllic part of the world became 'the enchanted place' where Christopher Robin and his friends had their adventures.

It was on a bridge over the river near Cotchford Farm that Christopher Robin and his bear played Poohsticks. The game, later celebrated in A.A. Milne's stories, consisted of dropping twigs into the fast-running water on the upstream side of the bridge and seeing whose twig was carried fastest on the current and emerged from under the bridge first.

So it was, that young Christopher Robin Milne, moved by small occurrences that were important to him from his life in London and the country, gave such an unlikely but memorable name to the bear who became the inspiration for the gentle adventures of a future record-breaking, international superstar – Winnie-the-Pooh.

The Pooh characters have since been redrawn by the Disney studio and there are now two distinct styles – classic Winnie-the-Pooh and Disney Winnie-the-Pooh. For those readers who like to get back to basics, many of Shepard's original drawings are on display at the Victoria & Albert Museum in London.

Another English bear whose fame has spread around the world is Paddington, who first appeared in 1958. Paddington is an independent bear, not a toy belonging to a small child, like Winnie-the-Pooh.

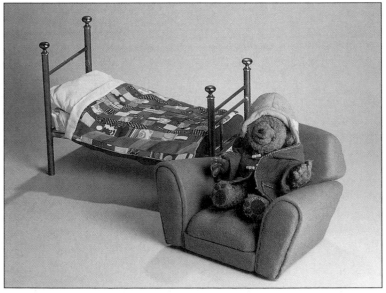

The original model of Paddington Bear made for the first animated television series, together with some of the props from the series.

Michael Bond, Paddington's creator, based him on a small bear he bought as a Christmas present for his first wife in December 1956. The Bond family lived close to Paddington station in west London, so Michael came up with the idea that the bear had been found there by a Mr and Mrs Brown. The young bear had been sent on the long journey from Peru to London by his Aunt Lucy, with a suitcase, a jar of marmalade and a label round his neck saying 'Please look after this bear. Thank you.'

Paddington is very much a bear of his times because his fame rocketed after he appeared on television in short films made using stop-go animation with small models of the bear. He is also a bear from a broken home – Michael Bond and his wife divorced and now share joint custody of Paddington. Like many hard-working celebrities Paddington puts his worldwide fame to good use and he and Michael Bond have actively supported the charity Action Research for more than twenty-five years.

Also a bear of his times is Sooty, one of the first stars of British children's television, and as popular today as when he first appeared in 1952. The original Sooty was a glove puppet

An early Sooty puppet, used by Sooty's creator Harry Corbett. The right paw is marked by the glue used to secure Sooty's magic wand.

by an unknown manufacturer, which was bought from a toy shop in 1948 by amateur magician Harry Corbett. The magician rubbed soot onto the puppet's ears and nose to give him his distinctive appearance and name. With Sooty as his special prop Harry Corbett made the decision to become a professional performer. To his surprise the teddy bear became the most popular thing in his show: 'The teddy quickly became the star and I was relegated to the role of his assistant.' Sooty was one of the first of the long line of stars – human and teddy bear – whose career was made by appearing on the exciting new medium of television. His TV show shot him to fame and Sooty puppets, made at that time by Chad Valley, were suddenly the latest craze.

Sooty was not quite the first teddy bear to appear on children's television. In 1950 the BBC introduced the popular puppet character Andy Pandy, who lived in a toy basket with his friend Looby Loo and a bear known simply as Teddy Bear.

Bears have been regulars on television ever since with stars like Big Ted of the long-running pre-school programme *Play School*, Super Ted and Pudsey Bear, who is the mascot of the annual BBC 'Children in Need' appeal.

One major way in which teddy has been celebrated throughout its first hundred years has been in music and song. The most success-ful teddy bear song ever written is 'The Teddy Bear's Picnic', which begins with the memorable words 'If you go down to the woods today you're sure of a big surprise!' The music was written by an American, John W. Bratton, and was first published in 1907 with the title 'The Teddy Bear Two-Step'. The tune enjoyed a certain degree of popularity,

> *Me and my Teddy Bear*
> *Got No Worries*
> *Got no Care*
> *Me and my Teddy Bear*
> *Just play and play all day.*

Song lyrics by Jack Winters and
J. Fred Coots, 1950

particularly as a circus theme, but it finally achieved classic status in 1930 when a British songwriter, Jimmy Kennedy, added the lyrics. The rest, as they say, is teddy bear history.

Countless songs have been written with a teddy bear theme. Among those which have displayed lasting qualities are 'Me and My Teddy Bear' and the Elvis Presley hit 'I Wanna Be Your Teddy Bear'. 'The Teddy Bear March', 'Dance of the Teddy Bears', 'Teddy Bear Rag', 'Teddy's Coming Home', 'There's Nothing Else But Teddy' and 'I Wish I Had a Teddy Bear' are just some of the titles that have enjoyed a fleeting moment of fame but are now forgotten. Many of the tunes were written in the first decade of the century when the USA was caught up in teddy bear fever.

Bears frequently make the leap from the printed page to the television or cinema screen and reach even wider audiences. The first teddy bear animated cartoon was made in 1909 and based on the newspaper strip 'Little

Johnny and the Teddy Bears' by John Randolph Bray, which had first appeared in 1907. In 1908 the Thomas A. Edison Company used stop-go animation with real teddy bears to make a short feature film. Walt Disney created his first screen teddy bear in 1924 in a film called *Alice and the Three Bears*. There is now a collection of much-loved teddy bear screencharacters, from Paddington to Winnie-the-Pooh himself. Although not strictly a teddy bear, Baloo the Bear made a great impression in the Disney animated film of Kipling's *The Jungle Book*. The Care Bears were created specifically for television and cinema, while the Muppet character Fozzie Bear and cartoon hero Super Ted both began life as television characters.

Nearly a century after the first songs, comic strips, films and books, teddy bears remain enduringly popular as subjects for stories and songs. New characters are created and new stories are published every year. The little bear with the big personality retains its hold on our imaginations, and the celebrations of teddy seem set to continue for many years to come.

EIGHT

The Rise and Rise of Edward Bear

The Great Teddy Bear Renaissance

At the beginning of the 1970s it looked as though the true traditional teddy bear was in danger of extinction. Ironically, its very popularity worked against its survival, as mass production threatened to turn a family of proud individuals with impressive names like Edward Bear, Growler, Theodore, Mr Bear, Theodosius, Archibald and Lady Elizabeth into mere conveyor-belt cuddly toys. Yet at the very moment when matters seemed at their lowest ebb and traditional teddy bear manufacturers everywhere were closing down, the seeds of the great teddy bear revival, also known as the teddy bear renaissance, were being sown.

Earlier generations of children who had found comfort in the friendship of their teddy bears were now parents and grandparents. Despite growing older, many of them still

Second World War evacuees leaving London with their teddy bears.

felt a strong affection for their bears, which was intensified by the childhood memories their faithful companions evoked. These 'bear-aware' adults were about to become the champions of the beleaguered traditional bear.

Although trends are hard to pin down, many people consider 1969 the year when the tide began to turn. It was in this year that Peter Bull, a larger-than-life British actor with his own collection of much-loved bears, published his landmark teddy bear book, *Bear With Me* (published in the USA as *The Teddy Bear Book*). Summing up the new attitude to the traditional bears of the past, Peter Bull wrote, 'In a genuine Teddy's face you see at once the loyalty, common sense and, above all, dependability behind it.'

The response the book evoked was quite overwhelming and totally unexpected. The author was inundated with letters from adult bear-lovers living in all corners of the globe. In confessing his own passion for teddies he had broken down the taboos that had prevented so many adults from feeling able to admit to a lasting and significant relationship with their own teddy bears. As Peter Bull himself observed, in an insight that may explain the phenomenal popularity of the teddy bear in the USA, 'Teddy Bears are so much cheaper than a psychiatrist and not nearly so supercilious.'

For the rest of his life Peter Bull was regarded as the ultimate authority on everything concerning teddy bears and was much in demand for television interviews and for appearances at any important teddy bear occasions. Wherever he went, throughout the world, his 3½-in tall miniature Steiff bear Theodore accompanied him, riding in his pocket. However, Theodore was not allowed to accompany Peter Bull when he went for tea with Theodore Roosevelt's daughter Alice Longworth to present her with a copy of *Bear With Me*. Mrs Longworth refused to let any bear in the house, declaring stoutly that she hated them.

Teddy bear pioneer Peter Bull pictured in a London square with some of the bears from his own collection.

Theodore, like his owner, was a regular television performer. In 1995, some years after Peter Bull's death, Theodore, with his personal effects, was sold for £14,625 ($23,000) – a lot of money for a little bear and a good illustration of how the provenance and history of a bear can add immeasurably to its value.

Bear watchers also attribute the revived popularity and wider appeal of the teddy bear to the tremendous success on both sides of the Atlantic of the 1981 television serial *Brideshead Revisited*. One of the main characters in the story, Sebastian Flyte, whose family lives in a magnificent stately home called Brideshead, has a bear called Aloysius,

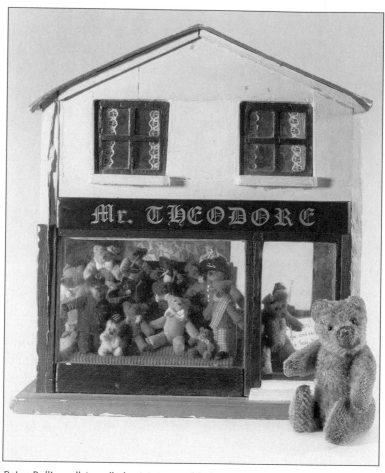

Peter Bull's well-travelled miniature teddy bear Theodore in front of his own teddy bear shop.

who is his constant companion. Although Sebastian Flyte is an adult he talks to his bear and treats him like a real person. This struck a chord with the millions of people who watched the television serial.

The bear used for filming was Delicatessen, one of the bears from Peter Bull's personal collection. Delicatessen is probably a 1907 Ideal Toy Company bear – a very rare bear indeed. Peter Bull named him Delicatessen because the bear had sat on a shelf in Ladd's Dry Goods Store, Saco, Maine, for over sixty years

Delicatessen as Aloysius, the teddy bear star of the television adaptation of *Brideshead Revisited*.

before being given to the actor by Mrs Euphemia Ladd, who had seen Peter Bull and his teddies on a television programme. Delicatessen took to acting with enthusiasm and his director praised him for never being late on the set, never being drunk and never bumping into his co-stars, who included Jeremy Irons, Anthony Andrews and Lord Olivier. So famous did Delicatessen become after all this television exposure that he eventually changed his name by deed poll to his stage name of Aloysius!

> ❝ What do you suppose Lord Sebastian wanted? A hairbrush for his Teddy-bear; it had to have very stiff bristles, not, Lord Sebastian said, to brush him with, but to threaten him with a spanking when he was sulky. ❞
>
> Evelyn Waugh,
> *Brideshead Revisited*, 1945

Ten years after Peter Bull's book was published, he was asked to help design a truly traditional teddy bear in accordance with all the best principles. This new, but old-fashioned, bear was manufactured by House of Nisbet, a British firm run by American Jack Wilson. The bear was named Bully Bear as a tribute to Peter Bull. Bully bears became an integral part of the House of Nisbet range and were produced in several variations including Captain Bully and Bully Minor. Peter Bull and Jack Wilson also designed another very successful teddy bear range called the Zodiac Bears, which reflected Peter Bull's own keen interest in astrology. In 1987 House of Nisbet made a replica Limited Edition of Peter Bull's most famous bear, Aloysius, the

star of the 1981 television adaptation of Evelyn Waugh's novel *Brideshead Revisited*. For copyright reasons (North American Bear Company had earlier made a version of Aloysius) this tribute bear reverted to the original name of Delicatessen. Sadly when Jack Wilson retired House of Nisbet stopped making bears and the Bully bears are no longer in production.

A further development in 1969, the year Peter Bull's influential book was published, was the launch of a charity called Good Bears of the World by an American journalist called Jim Ownby. The idea came to him as a direct result of Peter Bull's book, which proved to him that teddy bears were a potent force among adults as well as children and that this could be harnessed to do good. The charity's aim was simple – to raise money to buy teddy bears as a comfort for sick children (and adults) throughout the world.

In Britain there was already another rather unlikely teddy bear pioneer. Second-World-War veteran Colonel Bob Henderson had built up his own collection of over 500 bears and bear memorabilia, based around a 1904 Steiff bear called Teddy Girl, which had belonged to him and his brother when they were children. Teddy Girl (or a miniature teddy bear when the larger bear was not practical) had accompanied Colonel Henderson throughout the Second World War, acting as his good-luck mascot while he fought in North Africa. Colonel Henderson described the teddy bear as 'a silent symbol of love and understanding, so needed in the world today', and he spear-headed what he called 'Teddy Bear Consciousness' when he founded the Teddy Bear Club in 1962. Later he organised the British branch of Good Bears of the World and shares with Peter Bull and Jim Ownby the credit for raising the profile of the teddy bear during the 1970s.

THE MARQUESS OF BATH AND HIS TEDDY BEAR

The 6th Marquess of Bath, pictured at home with a furry friend, introduced the custom of holding large teddy bears' picnics at his stately home Longleat in Wiltshire. Since then, similar events have become popular all over the world, attracting hundreds of teddy bear enthusiasts and raising large sums for charity.

It was during the 1970s that bear-lovers and bear collecting acquired rather fanciful names based on the Greek for bear (*arctos*) and for lover (*philos*). The newly coined words were arctophile or arctophilist for someone who loves bears and arctophily or arctophilia for the hobby of collecting bears. Because the words are derived from Ancient Greek, they give the misleading impression that arctophily is a long-established pursuit rather than a comparatively new interest.

The custom of holding teddy bear rallies, teddy bear conventions and teddy bear picnics began to evolve during the late 1970s. Many of the early rallies were organised by Good Bears of the World to raise funds. Later the idea was used by a variety of different charities, most without any teddy bear connections, who saw it as a fun way of raising money for their cause while ensuring that their supporters enjoyed the occasion.

In 1979, the Marquess of Bath organised a Great Teddy Bear Rally at his stately home, Longleat, in Wiltshire. The rally lasted two days and was proof, if any were needed by this time, that by the end of the 1970s teddy bears were more popular with both adults and children than ever before.

The upsurge of interest in bears was the catalyst for saving the craft of making traditional teddy bears. Appropriately, since the USA claims to be the teddy bear's birthplace, the revival began in earnest on that side of the Atlantic. Collectors had begun to search out early bears for their attractive appearance and rarity value. From the early 1980s old teddy bears started to appear in sales in prestigious international auction houses like Sotheby's and Christie's. This was a sure sign that they were being taken

Marmaduke, a modern British bear styled in the traditional manner, designed in 1988 by Valerie Lyle of the British company Big Softies.

seriously as collectibles. But since there was a limited number of such bears available prices began to rise, putting them out of the reach of many bear-lovers. Collectors wanting similar bears at more affordable prices turned to the established makers, particularly those whose early bears were so sought after. They were not interested in mass-produced soft toys but in bears with the same features and hand-made quality that attracted them to the original toys. The result was that new, yet traditionally styled and made, teddy bears, were in demand again after a period of decline. The crucial difference this time was that manufacturers were making bears specifically for the adult collectors' market, and not just for children.

In the 1970s and early 1980s, before the revival had fully taken off in Britain itself, the British manufacturer Merrythought was creating designs, such as the 'E Bear' for American collectors. In 1990, with the American market in mind, it launched an International Collectors' Catalogue, which, as well as featuring reproductions of earlier bears, included new traditionally styled bears designed by Jackie Revitt.

Also in 1990 Dean's, under new ownership, reorganised itself and reflected the new emphasis on old-fashioned bears by reverting to the name Dean's Rag Book Company. Like other long-established firms, it opted out of competing with mass manufacturing and consolidated as a company specialising in high-quality, traditionally made bears. The same path was being followed in the USA by Gund and in Germany by Steiff and Hermann.

The latest generation of bears is now being made with the original features that gave them so much character in the first place. They are of high-quality mohair plush, usually in an authentic bear-like shade. Of British bears,

A hug of three 1980s straw-filled bears made by the Scottish company Atlantic Bears.

80 per cent are now made in various shades of gold, with the brighter 'London gold' being most popular, while in the USA traditional beige and brown or, perversely, very bright bears predominate. The new bears are jointed and often have humps like their forebears. Their snouts are more prominent and many of them growl. Their stuffing is firm and may even be wood-wool, as used in the very early bears. By using wood-wool as stuffing it achieves the stiff, upright appearance of the lovely pre-1914 bears, which are still the most prized by collectors. Except that very few original bears have survived in perfect condition, it would be hard to tell some of the new collectors' bears from those made nearly a hundred years ago.

There are several different ways in which the collectors' market has been developed and catered for. These include new traditionally styled bears, replicas, revivals, annivers-ary bears, artists' bears and limited editions.

William Shakesbear, a limited edition made by Steiff in the 1980s as a replica of their 1906 design.

Replica bears, made from existing old patterns kept in company archives, or copied from old bears, are much sought after. This has been a highly successful route for Steiff which has a meticulously maintained archive where all the patterns are kept on file.

Each year Steiff makes a limited number of bears from designs that were popular or rare in the past. Examples of Steiff replicas are Teddy Baby and Teddy Rose, a copy of a 1925 pink plush bear. It also makes replicas of individually well-known bears like the rare, red bear, Alfonzo. Where patterns do not exist they are reinvented, as House of Nisbet did so successfully with its replica of Delicatessen.

Berlin Bear, a 1990 limited edition by German company Hermann Teddy Original to commemorate the end of the Berlin Wall in 1989.

Long-established firms create 'anniversary bears' to celebrate significant milestones in their history, such as Hermann's Seventy-Fifth Anniversary Bear, brought out in 1990, the same year in which Merrythought produced its own Diamond Jubilee Bear.

Individual bear artists, usually working from home, design bears that are made entirely by hand, without using even the limited mechanisation employed by larger firms. The USA and Britain have a large number of such bear artists, working as individuals and selling most of their work through mail order or at teddy bear and craft fairs. Among the best-known British teddy bear artists are Naomi Laight, June Kendall, Shirley Latimer and Sue Clark. In the USA,

Limited edition bears made in 1993 by Welsh bear artist Sue Schoen.

where many bear artists flourish, Dee Hockenberry, Sue Foskey and Sue Lain are known for their delightfully individual bears.

Working on a larger scale are the new firms set up to meet the increased demand. These include British manufacturers like Nonsuch (established in 1979) and Canterbury Bears (established in 1980) and, in the USA, the North American Bear Company (established in the mid-1970s) and Applause (which began making its own bears in 1985).

Both large firms and bear artists create limited editions of specific designs, which, in their turn, become much sought after because of their rarity value. A large firm with a production line, like Steiff, might make a limited edition of several thousands. In contrast, bear artists who make the entire bear themselves soon feel the urge to move on to new challenges, and it is not uncommon for them to make limited editions of as few as five or ten, or even to create one-of-a-kind designs.

So great has been the success of the traditional teddy bear revival that countries in the Far East, which mass produced the cuddly toy versions, are now mass producing their own traditionally styled bears. There is also a growing tradition of Japanese artists' bears, made by both

Three bears made by Merrythought for the hundredth anniversary of the teddy bear. Above: President Roosevelt and bear cub. Right: 21st Century Cheeky.

men and women, often dressed in fantastical clothes. Japan, once known only for its fabric-covered, mechanical tin bears, now has its own teddy bear museum in Izu. Among the bears on display is Teddy Girl, the star of Colonel Bob Henderson's collection. So, after an uncertain period in teddy bear history, the wheel has come full circle, and the teddy bear's influence is stronger than ever. On his hundredth birthday teddy's paw print is firmly stamped on more countries than ever before.

NINE

Old Gold

Collecting Bears for Profit and Pleasure

Arctophilia, the new word for teddy bear collecting, is beginning to creep into the dictionaries, giving this pleasing, gentle hobby a new air of importance. Unfortunately, a higher profile also means increased prices as dealers begin to dominate a market that was once a cosy little world of people who loved bears for their own sake, not for the high prices they now fetch in the auction house.

The days of picking up bargains and making exciting discoveries have largely gone. Collecting teddy bears is becoming an increasingly expensive business. Since it is no longer possible to buy an example of every teddy bear design, collectors now have to specialise, as they do in other areas of collecting. For some people nothing will ever compare with the unique appeal of the very earliest bears, made in the pioneering years between 1903 and 1914.

But the cost of such bears is now measured in thousands, or even hundreds of thousands of pounds. Colonel Bob Henderson's Teddy Girl, a rare 1904 Steiff that was the star of his considerable collection, sold at auction following his death in 1994 for an amazing £110,000 ($168,000). It was bought by the Japanese collector Mr Sekiguchi for his new teddy bear museum in Izu. Such prices put the prestigious early bears out of the reach of most bear lovers. It would not be unusual today for a Steiff bear of this age and quality to fetch at least £5,000 at auction, even where there is no entertaining history or provenance.

Advertisement for Dean's Bri-Nylon bear with safety eyes. An excellent example of the washable bears being made in easy-care fabrics during the 1950s and 1960s.

A 1920s bear by J.K. Farnell with trademark silky plush and large glass eyes.

It is more realistic to choose a broader area if you want to build your own collection. Bears from the golden age between the wars are also enchanting and there are many more of them, so they are cheaper. Many of the bears referred to in this book, such as Schuco Yes/No bears or Chiltern Hugmee bears, are examples of prized bears from this period.

Some enthusiasts collect miniature bears from all periods; others choose to collect dressed bears, novelty bears – such as purses and muffs – or bears in bright mohairs. If you believe that koalas, pandas and polar bears count as teddy bears – though many enthusiasts insist they do not – you could make a collection of them.

Another possibility is to buy artists' bears, perhaps specialising in one particular artist. Collecting bears by one single manufacturer – especially one that still makes bears today, such as Steiff or Hermann in Germany, Gund in the USA or Dean's or Merrythought in Britain – makes it possible to build a collection from across the range of old and new. Alternatively it is possible to collect the quality antiques of the future by focusing on the fine reproductions of classic bears that manufacturers and bear artists have

been creating since the great teddy bear revival began in the early 1980s. To preserve their value, all new bears should be kept in mint condition, preferably in their boxes.

Mechanical bears make an interesting area of specialisation

A pull-along bear made in Germany in about 1910.

A Japanese mechanical bear, made from tin covered with acrylic fur in about 1950.

but they, too, can be expensive. Most of the major manufacturers made mechanical bears at some point, from the famous Steiff wind-up Tumbling Bear introduced in 1909, to the battery-operated toys made by Pedigree, including their walking Rupert Bear. There are plenty of interesting modern mechanical bears such as Teddy Ruxpin, a bear made by the American toy company Mattel, which talks with the help of a cassette. Another American toy manufacturer, Hasbro, has a bear called Bingo which talks when it is cuddled.

Japan and Russia, two countries that are not known for quality traditional bears (although Japan did make cheap bears from the 1920s onwards), nevertheless have a reputation for collectible mechanical bears. Constructed from fabric-covered tin, these toys did everything from playing the balalaika to eating ice-cream while walking along or turning the pages of a story book. Their clockwork mechanisms were not particularly strong, so they should be treated with extreme care.

As the previous chapters have revealed, Germany, the USA and Britain are the main centres of specialist teddy bear production, but other countries also have teddy bear firms and these could form an interesting area for collecting. The First World War stimulated a small teddy bear industry in Holland and in France when German bears became unavailable. French bears from this period tend to have long, thin bodies and large ears perched right on top of their heads. French firms used button trade-

A typical French bear of the 1920s, with limbs attached by pin jointing.

marks, and names to look out for include PF (Pintel Fils), FADAP (Fabrique Artistique d'Animaux en Peluche) – both companies made bears from the 1920s to the 1970s – and Jan Jac, whose best-known bears were made in the 1950s.

Australia now has several interesting bear artists but those wanting to collect early Australian bears should particularly search out Joy Toy Company bears, which were made from 1920 by a company that had already established itself as a maker of other types of toys. Not surprisingly, many Australian bears were made from sheepskin. Other Australian companies to look out for, all of which ceased trading in the 1970s and 1980s when faced with competition from cheap imports, are Emil Toys, Verna Toys and Berlex Company.

However you decide to structure your collection, make sure you are as well informed as possible by visiting teddy bear collections in specialist museums such as The Teddy Bear Museum in Stratford-upon-Avon, England, or The Teddy Bear Museum at Naples in Florida. Museums of dolls or childhood, like the Museum of Childhood in Edinburgh, Scotland, and the Museum of Childhood at Bethnal Green in London, England, are also full of interest for collectors who want to know more about how teddy bears fit into the history of childhood toys and toy collecting.

Your knowledge can also be built up by attending teddy bear auction sales and learning from the catalogue details which have been written by experts. You will develop an instinct for what bears are worth by noting the prices they fetch at auction. It is also worth visiting the teddy bear fairs that are held in towns and cities all over the world, where you will see a wide variety of bears and have the opportunity to talk to experienced makers and collectors. Fairs are an excellent way to meet bear artists and find the latest limited editions as well as stalls selling old bears. Another way to keep up-to-date with new developments is to join collectors' clubs, like those run by Merrythought and Dean's. These clubs produce magazines packed with interesting information as well as making new bears available to members.

Many excellent books have been published that document teddy bear history, how they are made and what they are worth. By reading these you will pick up useful hints to help you identify and date teddy bears you are thinking of buying. You will also learn what makes a bear special. For example, a small number of the pre-1914 Steiff bears were

Barbara Cartland's early twentieth-century bear 'The Prince of Love'.

made with a central seam down the middle of the face. This was an economy measure as six complete bears could be cut from a roll of mohair. With the left-over fabric a seventh was made which needed a seam down the middle of its head. Bears with a central seam fetch more money at auction than their exact counterparts made from one piece of fabric.

Knowing about dating is very important if you are going to be a serious collector. Trademarks and labels are fundamental clues to dating; for example, very early Steiff ear buttons carried a picture of an elephant and not, until 1905, the name Steiff.

Another important factor in collecting teddy bears is provenance – where the bear or teddy bear collectible comes from – and the proof of provenance – documents like letters and photographs – add enormously to the

COLLECTORS' CLUES

Small details can tell you a great deal about the history and age of a bear, and this list gives you a few clues.

- Early British firms J.K. Farnell and W.J. Terry and, later on, Merrythought, used the unusual 'webbed' style of stitching the 'claws'. This meant adding a horizontal line to link up the stitched claws to form a sort of blanket stitch along the bears' pads.
- Merrythought bears have only four stitched claws while early J.K. Farnell bears have five claws.
- When Dean's introduced a 'growler' into their bears it worked by being tipped forwards, not backwards like other firms' bears.
- The early American firm the Aetna Toy Animal Company was only in business from 1906–8. Its bears are therefore very rare. Aetna bears had the trademark Aetna stamped across the centre of the left foot.
- Early bears, up to about 1920, made by the Ideal Novelty and Toy Company (the firm founded by Morris and Rose Michtom) have feet which taper to a point.
- Almost all early bears were made of top-quality mohair.
- An unusual or inferior fabric such as cotton-rayon is a good indication that a bear was made during or just after the Second World War, when fabrics were rationed.
- Artificial silk plush, a feature of many early Merrythought bears, is typical of the 1930s.

- Pastel shades are an indication that a bear was made in the 1930s.
- Many very early bears have felt pads.
- Early Steiff bears will have red felt under their paw pads.
- The nose stitching helps identify bears. For example, Steiff stitching on small bears is horizontal but on larger bears it is vertical.
- Some classic Bing bears have a distinctive shield-shaped nose with five long central stitches extending down to a V-shaped mouth.
- The earliest bears had eyes made from black boot buttons.
- Glass eyes usually indicate a bear made after about 1920. Some early British bears are an exception to this rule.
- Plastic eyes were introduced in the early 1950s.

authenticity and value. This is particularly relevant in the world of teddy bears, where so few of the early bears retain their original labels and trademarks. It has become even more significant now that so many bears are again being made in the old-fashioned style. It is quite possible to 'age' these new bears in a way that can fool an inexperienced collector.

Attention to details like these can help you to buy wisely and enable you to identify a really special bear if the

Arden, an early British bear, possibly produced by J.K. Farnell, pictured with his young owner Claire Jukes, *c.* 1913. Inset: the same bear nearly ninety years later.

opportunity arises. There are many, many more fascinating facts you can learn about the world of collectible bears and you can be quite sure that all your homework will pay off and make you better prepared to recognise both a bargain and a fake.

To help you with your research, as well as books there are magazines such as *Teddy Bear Scene*, *Teddy Bear Times*, *Teddy Bear and Friends* and handbooks such as *Hugglets UK Teddy Bear Guide*. In them you will find listings of teddy bear shops, museums, manufacturers, bear artists, collectors' clubs – in short, everything of interest to the serious collector.

Although most people will want to collect actual teddy bears there are other teddy bear items that are also highly attractive to collectors. Two of these key areas are books and illustrations. First editions of the Winnie-the-Pooh stories fetch particularly high prices. Out of the reach of the pockets of most individual collectors and small museums are the original drawings made by E.H. Shepard for the Winnie-the-Pooh books. These now sell for many tens of thousands of pounds.

Also very collectible are copies of Seymour Eaton's *Roosevelt Bears* books, first editions of the early Paddington books and old copies of the Rupert collections and annuals. The early Rupert annuals are particularly popular with collectors. In 1996 a mint copy of the Rupert annual for 1936 was sold for a record price of £1,610 ($2,205).

A hand-knitted British bear, early 1990s.

Although Rupert is now world famous for his yellow-and-black checked trousers and scarf and his red sweater, some the earliest illustrations show him in a blue sweater and with blue-and-white checked trousers and scarf. Books with these differently coloured illustrations are highly

> A row of teddy bears sitting in a toyshop, all one size, all one price. Yet how different each one is from the next. Some look gay, some look sad. Some look stand-offish, some look loveable, and one over there has a specially endearing expression. Yes, that is the one I would like please.
>
> **Christopher Milne,**
> *The Enchanted Places,* 1974

prized. Facsimile copies of the early annuals appear regularly in limited editions and are now becoming collectible in their own right.

But despite all the hype and hysteria of the last few years the most important advice of all for true bear lovers continues to be to buy each bear not for what you think it might be worth, but because it pleases you – because the expression on its face says 'Please Buy Me'. That way, whatever the eventual value of your bear turns out to be in the harsh commercial world, to you it will always be an enchanting friend, and worth every penny you paid for it.

❝ Exit, pursued by a bear. ❞

Stage direction from William Shakespeare's
The Winter's Tale, 1611

The teddy bears' wedding reception. A selection of 1980s British artists' bears on display at The Teddy Bear Museum, Stratford-upon-Avon.

Teddy Bear Information

Compiled in association with Teddy Bear Scene
magazine

TEDDY BEAR RESTORERS

Britain

JOHN & KATHLEEN ANDERSON · 52 Ambleside Avenue · Seaham ·
Co Durham SR7 OHU
Telephone: 0191 581 5099
E-mail: john.jats@lineone.net

JACQUELINE EVANS · Bath Teddy Bear Clinic · Garden Studio · 5 Princes
Buildings · George Street · Bath BA1 2ED
Telephone: 01225 445803

BEAR LEE COTTAGE · 'Minto' · Codmore Hill · Pulborough · West Sussex
RH20 1BQ
Telephone: 01798 872707

BRIAN'S BEAR HOSPITAL · 76 Shortwood Avenue · Staines · Middlesex
WR12 7AJ
Telephone: 01784 451631

MAUREEN MARTIN · The Dolls' House · Stonehall Common · Worcester
WR5 3QQ
Telephone: 01905 820792
E-mail: MMBearDoll@aol.com

USA

THE DOLLS' HOSPITAL · 787 Lexington Avenue · New York NY 10021
Telephone: 001 212 838 7527

TEDDY BEAR MUSEUMS

Britain

ALICE'S WONDERLAND · Brougham Hall · Penrith · Cumbria
Telephone: 01768 895648
Doll and Teddy Museum open Easter–31 October; over 100 teddies, 1908–2000.

THE BEAR MUSEUM · 38 Dragon Street · Petersfield · Hampshire GU31 4JJ
Telephone: 01730 265108
Website: www.bearmuseum.co.uk

BETHNAL GREEN MUSEUM OF CHILDHOOD · Cambridge Heath Road ·
Bethnal Green · London E2 9PA
Telephone: 020 8980 2415
E-mail: BGMC@vam.ac.uk
Website: www.museumofchildhood.org.uk
*Outpost of the Victoria & Albert Museum. Open 10–5.50, closed all day Friday. About
120 early bears in the museum's collection of which roughly half are on display.*

BRITISH BEAR COLLECTION *(formerly Scotland's Teddy Bear Museum)* · Banwell
Castle · Banwell · Somerset BS29 6NX
Telephone: 01934 822263

THE BROADWAY EXPERIENCE · 76 High Street · Broadway · Worcestershire
WR12 7AJ
Telephone: 01386 858323
E-mail: bearsanddolls@hotmail.com
Website: www.jks.org/broadwaybearsanddolls.html

DORSET TEDDY BEAR MUSEUM · Teddy Bear House · Antelope Walk ·
Dorchester · Dorset DT1 1BE
Telephone: 01305 263200
Website: www.teddybearhouse.co.uk

HAMILTON TOY COLLECTION · 111 Main Street · Callander · Perthshire ·
Scotland FK17 8BQ
Telephone: 018773 30004
Open Easter–end of October

MERRYTHOUGHT TEDDY BEAR SHOP · Dale End · Ironbridge · Telford ·
Shropshire TF8 7NJ
Telephone: 01952 433029
E-mail: contact@merrythought.co.uk
Website: www.merrythought.co.uk
*Owned by Merrythought and just down the road from the factory. Vintage
Merrythought toys on display in the shop.*

THE RUPERT GALLERY · Canterbury Heritage Museum · Stour Street ·
Canterbury CT1 2JE
Telephone: 01227 452747
*Displays about Rupert and his creator Mary Tourtel in Mary Tourtel's home city.
For further information about Rupert contact:*
SHIRLEY REEVES · Membership Secretary · The Followers of Rupert ·
St Whitely · Windsor · Berkshire SL4 5PJ
Website: www.ee.ed.ac.uk/-afm/followers/

TEDDY BEARS OF WITNEY · 99 High Street · Witney · Oxfordshire OX8 6LY
Telephone: 01993 702616
E-mail: ordersonly@witneybears.co.uk
Website: www.teddybears.co.uk
*Really a shop but with a small collection of interesting bears including two of Peter
Bull's original bears, Delicatessen (Aloysius in the TV adaptation of Brideshead
Revisited) and Theodore, the miniature bear he took with him everywhere.*

THE TEDDY BEAR MUSEUM · 19 Greenhill Street · Stratford-upon-Avon ·
Warwickshire CV37 6LF
Telephone: 01789 293160
E-mail: info@theteddybearmuseum.com
Website: www.theteddybearmuseum.com
*Many hundreds of enchanting old and new bears, displayed in a house once
owned by King Henry VIII. Museum and shop open every day of the year except
25 and 26 December.*

TOY AND TEDDY BEAR MUSEUM · 373 Clifton Drive North · St Annes ·
Lancashire FY8 2PA
Telephone: 01253 713705

Ireland

TED'S ECLECTIC LOT · Haggard Street · Trim · County Meath · Eire
Telephone: 00 353 46 36263
E-mail: teds@eircom.net
Website: www.tedseclecticlot.ie
Open Tuesday to Saturday 11–6.

USA

AUNT LEN'S DOLL AND TOY MUSEUM · 6 Hamilton Terrace · New York
NY 10031
Telephone: 001 212 926 4172

CENTRAL CHILDREN'S ROOM · The Donnell Library Center · New York
Public Library · 20 West 53rd Street · New York NY 10019
Telephone: 001 212 704 8643
Has the original Winnie-the-Pooh and friends on display.

MARGARET WOODBERRY STRONG MUSEUM · 1 Manhattan Square ·
Rochester NY 14607
Telephone: 001 716 263 2700
Website: www.strongmuseum.org

TEDDY BEAR MUSEUM OF NAPLES · 2511 Pine Ridge Road · Naples FL 34109
Telephone: 001 941 598 2711
E-mail: info@teddymuseum.com
Website: www.teddymuseum.com

THEODORE ROOSEVELT BIRTHPLACE · 28 East 20th Street · New York NY 10003
Telephone: 001 212 260 1616
E-mail: MASISuperintendent@nps.gov
Website: www.nps.gov/thrb/index.htm

Germany

MARGARETE STEIFF MUSEUM · Alleenstrasse 2 · D-89537 Giengen (Brenz)
Telephone: 00 49 7322 1311
Situated inside the Steiff factory complex on the original site at Giengen.

TEDDYMUSEUM KLINGENBERG · Herr König In der Altstadt 7 · 63911
Klingenberg
Telephone: 00 49 9372 921167

Japan

IZU TEDDYBEAR MUSEUM · 1064–2 Yahatano · Ito-Shi · Shizuoka Prefecture
413-0232
Telephone: 00 81 557 545001

NASU TEDDYBEAR MUSEUM · 1185–4 Takakuhei Nasu-Machi · Nasu-Gun ·
Tochigi Prefecture 325-0302
Telephone: 00 81 287 761980

HAKONE TEDDYBEAR MUSEUM · 143–1 Motohakone Hakone-Machi ·
Ashigarashimo-Gun · Kanagawa Prefecture 250-0522
Telephone: 00 81 460 623111

South Korea

CHEJU TEDDY BEAR MUSEUM · Chungmun · Cheju Island · Seogwipo · South Korea
Website: www.teddybearmuseum.com

Switzerland

PUPPENHAUSMUSEUM BASEL · Steinevorstadt 1 · CH-4051 Basel
Telephone: 00 41 61 225 9595
Website: www.puppenhausemuseum.ch
Open Daily from 11–5, Thursdays until 8.

FAIRS AND EVENTS

Britain

THE EVENT
End of October at Alexandra Palace, London. About 200 stands of artist, antique and manufactured bears, bear-a-bilia, books, magazines, awards, special guests, talks and more. Exhibitors from all over the world.

THE MIDLANDS TEDDY EVENT
End of May at N.A.C. Stoneleigh Park, Coventry. The only 'Bear Artist Only' show in the country.

For details of both the above contact:
EMF PUBLISHING · 5–7 Elm Park · Ferring · West Sussex BN12 5RN
Telephone: 01903 244900
E-mail: info@dolltedemf.com
Website: www.dolltedemf.com

BIG TEDDY BEAR SHOW
End of April at the Business Design Centre, Islington, London.

BRITISH BEAR FAIR
December at Hove Town Hall, near Brighton, Sussex.

For details of both the above contact:
ASHDOWN PUBLISHING · Avalon Court · Star Road · Partridge Green · West Sussex RH13 8RY
Telephone: 01403 711511
E-mail: info@teddybeartimes.com
Website: www.teddybeartimes.com

HUGGLETS TEDDY BEAR FAIRS
Four fairs held in February, May, August and November at Kensington Town Hall, Kensington High Street, London.

For details of the above and of their local teddy bear fairs, including Stratford-upon-Avon, contact:
HUGGLETS
PO Box 290 · Brighton · East Sussex BN2 1DR

Telephone: 01273 697974
E-mail: Info@hugglets.co.uk
Website: www.hugglets.co.uk

MINIATURA
Held in April and November at the NEC Birmingham. For details contact:
41 Eastbourne Avenue · Hodge Hill · Birmingham B34 6AR
Telephone: 0121 749 7330

CHARITIES

Britain

ACTION RESEARCH (Paddington's Action Club) · Vincent House · North
Parade · Horsham · West Sussex RH12 2DP
Telephone: 01403 210406
Website: www.paddingtonsworld.co.uk
Funds research into childhood disabilities.

WORLD SOCIETY FOR THE PROTECTION OF ANIMALS (WSPA) · 89 Albert
Embankment · London SE1 7TP
Telephone: 020 7793 0540
E-mail: wspa@wspa.org.uk
Website: www.wspa.org.uk
Donations to:
WSPA · Freepost SCE6686 · Melksham SN12 6CZ
Freephone: 0800 316966
*Campaigns against ill-treatment of bears worldwide, including bear-baiting and
bear 'farming' for gall bile for use as an aphrodisiac.*

LIBEARTY · Jonathan Owen
Telephone: 0207 587 5019
E-mail: Jonathanowen@wspa.org.uk
Website: www.wspa.org.uk
*WSPA's specific campaign to save real live bears which are being ill-treated around
the world.*

PUBLICATIONS

Britain

TEDDY BEAR SCENE & OTHER FURRY FRIENDS · EMF Publishing · EMF House ·
5–7 Elm Park · Ferring · West Sussex BN12 5RN
Telephone: 01903 244900
E-mail: info@dolltedemf.com

Website: www.dolltedemf.com
Bi-monthly full-colour publication featuring, modern, antique and manufactured bears. Exclusive editorial, in-depth interviews, show and museum reports, paw post and competitions. Editor, Jennie Alexander, often chats online in a bear chat room: www.network54.com/hide/chat/55774.

TEDDY BEAR TIMES · Ashdown Publishing Limited · Avalon Court · Star Road · Partridge Green · West Sussex RH13 8RY
Telephone: 01403 711511
E-mail: support@ashdown.co.uk
Website: www.teddybeartimes.com
Monthly colour magazine.

TEDDY BEAR CLUB INTERNATIONAL · Aceville Publications Ltd · Castle House · 97 High Street · Colchester · Essex CO1 1TH
Telephone: 01206 505950
E-mail: sharon@aceville.com
Website: www.planet-teddybear.com
Monthly colour publication.

WONDERFUL WORLD OF TEDDY BEARS · De Agostini UK Ltd · Griffin House · 161 Hammersmith Road · London W6 8SD
Website: www.world-of-teddy-bears.com
Fortnightly part work.

Germany

BÄRREPORT · Venloer Strasse 686 · 50827 Cologne
Telephone: 00 49 22 1530 5567
E-mail: baerreport@netcologne.de
Website: www.baerreport.de
Quarterly full-colour publication in German language.

Netherlands

TEDDY-BEER · Uitgeverij Niesje Wolters van Bemmel · Centrumweg 8 · 8162 PT Epe
Telephone: 00 31 578 620502
E-mail: info@niesjewolters.nl
Website: www.niesjewolters.nl

USA

TEDDY BEAR AND FRIENDS · 6405 Flank Drive · Harrisburg PA 17112
Telephone: 001 717 657 9555

Website: www.teddybearandfriends.com
Bi-monthly.

TEDDY BEAR REVIEW · 1107 Broadway · Ste. 1210 N · New York NY 10010
Telephone: 001 212 989 8700
Website: www.teddybearreview.com
Bi-monthly.

Canada

CANADIAN TEDDY BEAR NEWS · Box 457 · Water Valley · Alberta T0M 2E0
Website: www.teddybearnews.com
Quarterly black and white.

Japan

TEDDY BEAR TIMES JAPAN · Ashdown Publishing Japan · 2–16–301 Uchida-machi · Ashiya-shi · Hyogo-ken 659-0022
Telephone: 00 81 7 9738 1660
Fax: 00 81 7 9738 1644
Six issues a year.

JAPAN TEDDY BEAR FAN CLUB · Japan Teddy Bear Co. · 1-36-4 Senriyama-nichi · Suita-shi · Osaka 565-0851
Telephone: 00 81 6 6330 9595
Fax: 00 81 6 6330 9494
Six issues a year.

TEDDY BEAR VOICE · Japan Teddy Bear Association · 10–14 Sarugaku-cho #201
Shibuya-ku · Tokyo 150-0033
Telephone: 00 81 3 3770 8539
Fax: 00 81 3 3770 8456
Six issues a year.

SHOPS, AUCTION HOUSES AND COLLECTORS' CLUBS

There are now so many teddy bear shops throughout the world, including those at the museums, that it would be impossible to mention them all. Magazines like *Teddy Bear Scene* and *Hugglets* have many advertisements which will help you locate a teddy bear shop near you where you can find modern teddy bears by traditional manufacturers like Steiff, Hermann, Gund, Merrythought and Dean's. If you are looking for an old bear, then an auction house is a good place to start. There are also several well-established shops that specialise in selling old bears and deal internationally.

Britain

THE BEAR FACTORY · 6th Floor · 2 Fouberts Place · London W1F 7PA
Telephone: 020 7479 7393
Website: www.bearfactory.co.uk

THE ENGLISH TEDDY BEAR COMPANY · 8 Belmont · Lansdowne Road · Bath BA1 5DZ
Telephone: 0845 6022739
Website: www.teddy.co.uk

ASQUITHS UNITED KINGDOM OF TEDDY BEARS · 2–4 New Street · Henley on Thames · Oxon RG9 2BT
Telephone: 01491 571978
Website: www.asquiths.com

THE DEAN'S COLLECTORS' CLUB · The Dean's Rag Book Company Ltd · Pontypool · Gwent · Wales NP4 6YY
Telephone: 01495 764881
Website: www.deansbears.com

MERRYTHOUGHT INTERNATIONAL COLLECTORS' CLUB · Ironbridge · Telford · Shropshire TF8 7NJ
Telephone: 01952 433116
Website: www.merrythought.co.uk

SUE PEARSON DOLLS & TEDDY BEARS · 131/2 Prince Albert Street · The Lanes · Brighton · East Sussex BN1 1HE
Telephone: 01273 329247
E-mail: enquire@sue-pearson.co.uk
Website: www.sue-pearson.co.uk

BONHAMS AUCTIONEERS (Chelsea) · 65–69 Lots Road · London SW10 0RN
Telephone: 020 7393 3900
Website: www.bonhams.com

CHRISTIE'S AUCTIONEERS · 85 Old Brompton Road · London SW7 3LD
Telephone: 020 7581 7611
Website: www.christies.com

SOTHEBY'S AUCTIONEERS · 34–35 New Bond Street · London W1A 2AA
Telephone: 020 7293 5000
Website: www.sothebys.com

Select Bibliography

Axe, John. *The Magic of Merrythought*, Ironbridge, Merrythought, 1986

Brown, Michèle. *The Teddy Bear Hall of Fame*, London, Headline Books, 1996

Bull, Peter. *Bear with Me*, London, Hutchinson, 1969

——. *The Teddy Bear Book*, revised edn, Cumberland (Maryland, USA), Hobby House Press, 1987

Bull, Peter and Pauline McMillan. *The Zodiac Bears*, Winscombe, House of Nisbet, 1984

Cieslik, Jurgen and Marianne. *Button-in-Ear*, Jülich (Germany), Marianne Cieslik Verlag, 1989

Cockrill, Pauline. *The Ultimate Teddy Bear Book*, London, Dorling Kindersley, 1991

——. *The Teddy Bear Encyclopedia*, London, Dorling Kindersley, 1993

Hebbs, Pam. *Collecting Teddy Bears*, London, Collins, 1988

Hockenbury, Dee. *The Big Bear Book*, Atglen (Pennsylvania, USA), Schiffer Publishing, 1996

Milne, Christopher. *The Enchanted Places*, London, Eyre Methuen, 1974

——. *The Path Through the Trees*, London, Eyre Methuen, 1979

Pearson, Sue. *Teddy Bears*, London, De Agostini Editions, 1995

Stewart, Brian and Howard Smith. *The Rupert Bear Dossier*, London, Hawk Books, 1997

Thwaite, Anne. *A.A. Milne, His Life*, London, Faber & Faber, 1990

Tibballs, Geoff. *The Secret Life of Sooty*, Letchworth, Ringpress, 1990

Waugh, Evelyn. *Brideshead Revisited*, London, Chapman & Hall, 1945

Index